BANKING INTERVIEW QUESTIONS AND ANSWERS

(CRACKING THE BANKING INTERVIEW: ESSENTIAL QUESTIONS, EXPERT ANSWERS, AND PROVEN STRATEG

CHETAN SINGH

Made with ♥ on the Notion Press Platform
www.notionpress.com

Contents

Acknowledgements

I would like to express my sincere gratitude to all the individuals who have contributed to this book on banking interview questions and answers.

First and foremost, I would like to thank the banking professionals who shared their valuable insights and expertise, providing valuable information and guidance on what to expect during a banking interview. Their contributions have helped to make this book a comprehensive resource for anyone seeking a career in the industry.

I would also like to acknowledge the support and encouragement of my family, who have been with me every step of the way and believed in me even when I doubted myself.

Thank you all for your contributions and support, and I hope that this book will be a valuable resource for anyone seeking a career in banking.

CHAPTER ONE

The world of banking is dynamic, challenging, and rewarding. If you're looking to launch or advance your career in this exciting industry, it's essential to be well-prepared for your interview. Banking interviews can be complex and intimidating, with recruiters testing your knowledge of the industry and evaluating your skills and qualifications.

In this book, we've compiled a comprehensive collection of the most common banking interview questions, along with expert answers and insider tips to help you shine in your interview. We've also included a comprehensive glossary of banking terminology to help you expand your vocabulary and understand industry-specific language.

Whether you're a seasoned professional or just starting out in the banking world, this guide is an invaluable resource for your career growth and success. It will help you understand what recruiters are looking for and how to showcase your skills and qualifications effectively. So why wait? Start reading this book now, and get ready to ace your banking interview!.

CHAPTER TWO

Overview of the Banking Industry

The banking industry is a critical sector of the global economy, responsible for facilitating the flow of money and credit in the economy. Banks play a central role in many financial transactions, including the accepting of deposits, granting of loans, and providing various other financial services to individuals, businesses, and governments. The banking industry is regulated by governments around the world, and its stability and performance are critical for the overall health of the economy.

The banking industry has undergone significant changes in recent years, with the advent of digital technology and the growing importance of e-commerce and online banking. As a result, banks must keep pace with the rapidly evolving landscape and remain competitive in an increasingly digital world. This has led to increased competition and a growing focus on customer service, innovation, and risk management.

For individuals seeking a career in the banking industry, there are many opportunities to specialize in areas such as retail banking, corporate banking, investment banking, wealth management, and more. Regardless of the role, a strong foundation in finance, economics, and business is essential for success in the banking industry.

CHAPTER THREE

How to Use This Book

This book on Banking Interview Questions and Answers is designed to be a comprehensive guide for individuals preparing for a banking interview. The book can be used in a variety of ways to suit your individual needs and goals, including:

Study and Review: Use the book as a reference to review common banking interview questions and answers, along with expert tips and strategies. Review the glossary of banking terminology to expand your vocabulary and deepen your understanding of the industry.

Practice and Preparation: Use the book to practice your answers to common interview questions, and become more comfortable and confident in your responses. Utilize the tips and strategies outlined in the book to tailor your responses to the specific role and company you are interviewing with.

Research and Insight: Use the book to gain insight into what recruiters are looking for in a candidate and the skills and qualifications they value. This can help you tailor your resume, cover letter, and interview responses to better match the needs of the company.

Career Development: Use the book as a tool for your ongoing career development and growth in the banking industry. Stay up-to-date with the latest industry trends, and continue to expand your knowledge and skills.

By using this book in combination with your own research and preparation, you can become well-equipped to succeed in your banking interview and launch or advance your career in this exciting and dynamic industry.

CHAPTER FOUR

Banking Interview Questions and Answers

What motivated you to pursue a career in banking?

Answer: I have always been fascinated by the financial industry and the role it plays in the economy. I am particularly drawn to the banking sector because of its ability to provide individuals and businesses with the financial resources they need to grow and succeed. I believe that a career in banking would allow me to make a real impact in people's lives and help to build a stronger, more prosperous community.

What do you think are the key skills required for a successful career in banking?

Answer: Strong analytical and problem-solving skills, the ability to communicate effectively, and a deep understanding of financial products and services are all critical for success in a banking career. Additionally, the ability to build relationships and work well with a team is essential, as is the ability to adapt and stay current with changes in the industry.

How do you stay up-to-date with developments in the banking industry?

Answer: I stay up-to-date by reading industry publications and attending relevant conferences and seminars. I also network with other professionals in the industry and make sure to keep abreast of any new regulations or policies that may affect the banking sector.

What are your strengths and weaknesses?

Answer: My strengths include my analytical and problem-solving skills, my ability to communicate effectively, and my deep understanding of financial products and services. One of my weaknesses is that I can be a bit of a perfectionist and sometimes struggle to delegate tasks effectively. However, I am working on improving my ability to trust and empower my team members.

What would you like to achieve in your career in banking?

Answer: I would like to build a successful career in banking by developing a deep understanding of the industry and the needs of my clients. Ultimately, I would like to take on a leadership role within the organization and contribute to the growth and success of the bank.

Why do you want to work in the banking industry?

Answer: I have always been interested in the financial industry and the role it plays in the economy. The banking sector, in particular, appeals to me because of its ability to provide individuals and businesses with the financial resources they need to grow and succeed. I believe that a career in banking would allow me to make a real impact in people's lives and help to build a stronger, more prosperous community.

What experience do you have in the banking industry?

Answer: I have [X number] of years of experience working in [specific area of banking, such as retail banking, commercial banking, investment banking, etc.]. During that time, I have gained experience in [specific skills or tasks, such as underwriting loans, managing customer accounts, analyzing financial statements, etc.]. I have also completed [relevant education or training, such as a degree in finance or a banking certification program].

How do you stay current on developments in the banking industry?

Answer: I stay current by reading industry publications and attending relevant conferences and seminars. I also network with other professionals in the industry and make sure to keep abreast of any new regulations or policies that may affect the banking sector. Additionally, I constantly research and analyze financial products and services to understand their features and benefits, and how they can be used to meet customers‘ needs.

How do you handle difficult customers or clients?

Answer: I handle difficult customers or clients by remaining calm and professional at all times. I listen actively to understand their concerns, and then provide clear and concise information to address their issues. I also apologize for any inconvenience they may have experienced and take ownership of the problem to find a solution. I always strive to maintain a positive relationship with all customers and clients, even in challenging situations.

Can you give an example of a time when you had to make a difficult decision in a banking setting?

Answer: One time, I had to make a decision about whether to approve a loan for a small business that had some financial challenges. After analyzing the business's financial statements and projections, I determined that the business had a solid plan for recovery and a high likelihood of success. However, the business had a lower credit score than our bank's typical loan standards. I had to weigh the potential risk of approving the loan against the potential benefit to the community and the business. After evaluating all the information, I decided to approve the loan with certain conditions to mitigate the risk, and it ended up being a successful loan. It helped the small business to stay afloat during tough times and created jobs in the community.

How do you handle multiple tasks and priorities in a fast-paced banking environment?

Answer: I handle multiple tasks and priorities by staying organized and prioritizing my workload. I make a to-do list and set deadlines for myself to ensure that I stay on track and meet all of my responsibilities. I also use time management techniques such as the Pomodoro technique to increase my productivity. Additionally, I communicate effectively with my team and managers to ensure that I am aware of any urgent tasks or priorities that may arise.

How do you maintain confidentiality and protect sensitive information in the banking industry?

Answer: I maintain confidentiality and protect sensitive information by adhering to strict security protocols and procedures. I am familiar with banking regulations such as the Gramm-Leach-Bliley Act and the Bank Secrecy Act and make sure to comply with all of the necessary regulations. I also make sure to keep all customer and client information secure by utilizing encryption and secure storage methods. And I am always aware of the cyber threats, and I make sure to stay up-to-date with the latest security measures.

How do you build and maintain strong customer relationships in the banking industry?

Answer: I build and maintain strong customer relationships by providing excellent customer service and being responsive to their needs. I take the time to understand their financial goals and tailor my recommendations to meet those goals. I also keep in touch with my customers on a regular basis to ensure that their needs are being met and to identify any potential issues or opportunities. Additionally, I make sure to be transparent and honest in all of my interactions with customers, which helps to build trust and loyalty.

How do you handle a customer's complaint?

Answer: I handle a customer's complaint by staying calm and professional. I listen to the customer and try to understand their concerns. I apologize for any inconvenience they may have experienced, and I take ownership of the problem. I then investigate the issue and provide the customer with a clear and concise explanation of what went wrong, and what steps I will take to resolve the issue. I also follow up with the customer to ensure that their issue has been fully resolved to their satisfaction.

Why should we hire you?

Answer: You should hire me because I have the skills and experience necessary to excel in a banking role. I am knowledgeable about financial products and services, and I am able to analyze and evaluate financial information quickly and accurately. I am also able to communicate effectively and build strong relationships with customers and clients. Additionally, I am highly motivated and dedicated to the success of the bank and the customers it serves. I am committed to continuous learning and personal development, and I am sure that I will bring value to the organization.

How do you handle a high-stress situation in a banking environment?

Answer: I handle high-stress situations in a banking environment by remaining calm and focused. I prioritize tasks and stay organized to manage my workload effectively. I also communicate with my team and managers to ensure that I am aware of any urgent tasks or priorities that may arise. Additionally, I take breaks when necessary to clear my mind and re-energize. I also practice mindfulness techniques to keep my emotions in check and make rational decisions.

How do you ensure compliance with banking regulations?

Answer: I ensure compliance with banking regulations by staying informed about the latest laws and regulations, such as the Bank Secrecy Act, the Gramm-Leach-Bliley Act, and the Anti-Money Laundering laws. I also follow the bank's compliance policies and procedures, and I attend regular training sessions to ensure that I am up-to-date with the latest compliance requirements. I also report any suspicious activities or breaches of regulations to the appropriate authorities.

How do you manage and mitigate risk in a banking environment?

Answer: I manage and mitigate risk by conducting thorough assessments of potential risks and developing a risk management plan. I also implement controls and procedures to minimize potential risks and ensure compliance with regulations. I regularly review and update the risk management plan to reflect changes in the bank's operations or regulatory environment. Additionally, I communicate effectively with my team and managers to ensure that all staff members are aware of potential risks and the steps that need to be taken to mitigate them.

How do you deal with difficult colleagues or supervisors in a banking environment?

Answer: I deal with difficult colleagues or supervisors by maintaining a professional attitude and focusing on finding solutions to problems. I try to understand their perspective and communicate effectively to find common ground. I also bring any issues or concerns to the appropriate person, such as a manager or human resources representative, for resolution. If necessary, I also seek feedback and take responsibility for my actions, and I am willing to make necessary changes to improve relationships.

How do you stay motivated and engaged in a banking environment?

Answer: I stay motivated and engaged by setting goals for myself and working towards achieving them. I also take on new challenges and responsibilities to keep my work interesting. I keep learning about the industry and financial products and services to stay current and improve my skills. Additionally, I maintain a positive attitude and work well with my team to create a positive work environment. I also make sure to take breaks when necessary and engage in activities that I enjoy to maintain a good work-life balance.

How do you handle a situation where a customer wants to open an account, but they don't meet the bank's qualifications?

Answer: I handle this situation by being transparent and honest with the customer. I explain the bank's qualifications and the reason why they do not meet the requirements. I also offer them alternative solutions, such as a secured credit card or a savings account, that may help them to build their credit or savings. I also make sure to inform the customer about any government programs or non-profit organizations that may be able to assist them. I always want to make sure that the customer understands the reason for the decision and is aware of their options.

How do you manage and reconcile customer accounts?

Answer: I manage and reconcile customer accounts by ensuring that all transactions are recorded accurately and in a timely manner. I perform regular account audits, comparing account balances to bank records and identifying and resolving any discrepancies. I also make sure that customer account information is up-to-date and accurate. I review account activity for any suspicious or fraudulent activities and report any concerns to the appropriate authorities. Additionally, I communicate with customers to ensure that their account information is correct and that they understand their account balances and transactions.

How do you ensure compliance with the bank's policies and procedures?

Answer: I ensure compliance with the bank's policies and procedures by staying informed about the bank's policies and procedures, including the Code of Conduct. I also attend regular training sessions to ensure that I am up-to-date with the latest policies and procedures. I also follow the bank's compliance policies and procedures, and I report any breaches of policies or procedures to the appropriate authorities. Additionally, I communicate effectively with my team and managers to ensure that all staff members are aware of the bank's policies and procedures, and that they understand the importance of compliance.

How do you manage and analyze financial data?

Answer: I manage and analyze financial data by utilizing financial analysis tools such as spreadsheets and financial software. I also use financial ratios, trend analysis, and other techniques to identify trends, patterns, and opportunities in the data. I also make sure to validate the data and ensure that it is accurate and reliable. Additionally, I communicate effectively with my team and managers to ensure that the data is being used to make informed business decisions.

How do you ensure customer satisfaction in a banking environment?

Answer: I ensure customer satisfaction by providing excellent customer service and being responsive to their needs. I take the time to understand their financial goals and tailor my recommendations to meet those goals. I also keep in touch with my customers on a regular basis to ensure that their needs are being met and to identify any potential issues or opportunities.

Additionally, I make sure to be transparent and honest in all of my interactions with customers, which helps to build trust and loyalty. I also follow up with customers to ensure that they are satisfied with the services provided.

How do you handle and resolve disputes or complaints from customers?

Answer: I handle and resolve disputes or complaints from customers by staying calm and professional. I listen actively to understand the customer's concerns and apologize for any inconvenience they may have experienced. I take ownership of the problem and investigate the issue thoroughly. I provide the customer with clear and concise information to address their issues and take the necessary steps to resolve the issue to the customer's satisfaction. I also follow up with the customer to ensure that the issue has been fully resolved and that they are satisfied with the resolution.

How do you maintain a high level of security for customer account information?

Answer: I maintain a high level of security for customer account information by adhering to strict security protocols and procedures. I am familiar with banking regulations such as the Gramm-Leach-Bliley Act and the Bank Secrecy Act and make sure to comply with all necessary regulations. I also make sure to keep all customer and client information secure by utilizing encryption and secure storage methods. I also ensure that all employees are trained in security protocols and that they understand the importance of protecting customer information. Additionally, I stay updated with the latest security measures and make sure to implement them in the bank.

How do you ensure compliance with anti-money laundering (AML) regulations?

Answer: I ensure compliance with anti-money laundering (AML) regulations by staying informed about the latest laws and regulations, such as the Bank Secrecy Act, the Money Laundering Control Act, and the USA PATRIOT Act. I also follow the bank's

AML policies and procedures, and I attend regular training sessions to ensure that I am up-to-date with the latest AML requirements. I also report any suspicious activities or breaches of AML regulations to the appropriate authorities. Additionally, I communicate effectively with my team and managers to ensure that all staff members are aware of AML regulations and the steps that need to be taken to comply with them.

How do you identify and prevent fraud in a banking environment?

Answer: I identify and prevent fraud in a banking environment by staying informed about the latest fraud trends and techniques. I also perform regular account audits, comparing account balances to bank records and identifying and resolving any discrepancies. I review account activity for any suspicious or fraudulent activities and report any concerns to the appropriate authorities. Additionally, I communicate effectively with my team and managers to ensure that all staff members are aware of potential fraud risks and the steps that need to be taken to prevent them. I also inform customers about common fraud schemes and how to avoid them.

How do you stay up-to-date with the latest technology in the banking industry?

Answer: I stay up-to-date with the latest technology in the banking industry by attending relevant conferences and seminars, reading industry publications and by staying informed about new technologies that are being developed by other financial institutions. Additionally, I research and evaluate new technologies that have the potential to improve banking operations or provide new services to customers. I also communicate effectively with my team and managers to ensure that the bank is taking advantage of the latest technologies to improve its operations and meet the needs of its customers.

How do you manage a team in a banking environment?

Answer: I manage a team in a banking environment by setting clear goals and expectations, providing regular feedback, and promoting open communication. I lead by example and set a positive tone for the team. I also provide regular training and development opportunities to help my team members improve their skills and knowledge. I also delegate responsibilities effectively and empower my team members to make decisions and take ownership of their tasks. Additionally, I create a positive and inclusive work environment that promotes teamwork and collaboration.

How do you develop and maintain a sales pipeline in a banking environment?

Answer: I develop and maintain a sales pipeline by identifying potential customers and conducting research to understand their needs and financial goals. I then use that information to develop a sales strategy and approach that is tailored to their specific needs. I also use various sales techniques such as networking, cold calling, and email campaigns to generate leads and build relationships with potential customers. I also track and analyze my sales progress and adjust my strategy as needed to ensure that I am meeting my sales goals. Additionally, I maintain regular contact with my existing customers to ensure their satisfaction and identify any potential sales opportunities.

How do you assess creditworthiness and risk for loan applications?

Answer: I assess creditworthiness and risk for loan applications by conducting a thorough review of the applicant's financial information, including their credit history, income, and assets. I also consider any relevant information about the applicant's business or personal financial situation, such as their ability to repay the loan and their debt-to-income ratio. I also use various credit scoring models and risk assessment tools to evaluate the applicant's creditworthiness and risk level. Finally, I make a decision based on a combination of my analysis and judgement, taking into account the bank's lending policies and guidelines, as well as the applicant's specific financial situation.

How do you handle and manage loan portfolios?

Answer: I handle and manage loan portfolios by regularly reviewing and monitoring loan performance, ensuring that all loans are in compliance with bank policies and guidelines, and taking necessary actions to mitigate risk. I also maintain accurate loan records and ensure that loan documentation is complete and up-to-date. I also communicate effectively with loan officers, borrowers, and other stakeholders to address any issues or concerns that may arise. Additionally, I use various loan portfolio management tools and techniques to analyze loan performance, identify trends and risks, and make informed decisions to maximize loan portfolio returns.

Can you give an example of a time when you provided exceptional customer service?

Answer: I have had many opportunities to provide exceptional customer service in my career. One example that stands out to me is when I assisted a customer who had lost their debit card while traveling abroad. The customer was in a foreign country and had no access to their funds. I worked closely with the customer to quickly cancel their old card and issue a new one, and I also helped them to access emergency funds through a cash advance. The customer was extremely grateful for my help and left the bank with a positive impression. This experience taught me the importance of going above and beyond to help customers in need and the impact that it can have on building trust and loyalty.

How do you stay updated on changes in banking regulations and industry standards?

Answer: I stay updated on changes in banking regulations and industry standards by regularly reading industry publications, attending training and professional development sessions, and participating in industry events and conferences. I also maintain a network of professional contacts in the banking industry and seek their input and advice on important industry developments. Additionally, I stay informed about any changes or updates in banking regulations by monitoring relevant websites and subscribing to alerts and newsletters from regulatory bodies.

I stay informed about any changes or updates in banking regulations by monitoring relevant websites and subscribing to alerts and newsletters from regulatory bodies. I believe that staying informed and knowledgeable about changes in the banking industry is critical to providing effective and compliant banking services to my customers.

Can you describe a time when you had to handle a difficult customer situation?

Answer: I have had to handle a number of difficult customer situations in my career. One situation that stands out was when a customer came into the bank to dispute a charge on their account. The customer was upset and frustrated, and I had to remain calm and professional while I investigated the issue. After reviewing the account and the transaction, I discovered that the charge was legitimate and I had to explain this to the customer. I took the time to listen to the customer's concerns and explain the situation in a clear and concise manner. I also offered the customer alternative solutions to resolve the issue. By demonstrating empathy and a willingness to help, I was able to diffuse the situation and leave the customer feeling satisfied with the resolution.

Can you describe a time when you went above and beyond for a customer?

Answer: One example of when I went above and beyond for a customer was when a small business owner came to me for help with financing their expansion plans. The owner was turned down by multiple other banks and was feeling discouraged. I took the time to understand their business, their goals, and their financial situation, and I identified a unique solution that could help them secure the financing they needed. I then worked closely with the business owner to guide them through the application process and advocate for their loan with the bank's lending committee. The loan was approved and the business owner was able to expand their business and achieve their goals. The customer was grateful for my help and the extra effort I put into finding a solution for them.

How do you handle confidential information in a banking environment?

Answer: I handle confidential information in a banking environment by adhering to strict security protocols and policies. I understand the importance of protecting customer information and take every precaution to ensure that information is not disclosed improperly. This includes keeping confidential information secure and confidential, disposing of sensitive information properly, and only accessing information on a need-to-know basis. I also stay informed about the latest security trends and best practices in the industry and participate in regular security training to ensure that I am always following the best and most secure methods for handling confidential information.

Can you describe a time when you had to handle a sensitive issue with a customer?

Answer: One time, a customer came to me with a sensitive issue related to a mistake made on their account. The customer was upset and worried about the impact on their finances. I listened to the customer's concerns and investigated the issue thoroughly. I then worked with the customer to find a resolution that was fair and acceptable to both parties. I also kept the customer informed throughout the process and made sure that their information was kept confidential. By handling the issue in a professional and sensitive manner, I was able to build trust with the customer and demonstrate my commitment to providing the best possible service.

How do you prioritize tasks and manage your workload in a fast-paced banking environment?

Answer: In a fast-paced banking environment, it is important to prioritize tasks and manage my workload effectively. I prioritize tasks by setting clear goals and prioritizing tasks based on urgency, importance, and impact. I also use technology, such as task management software and calendars, to help me stay organized and track my progress. To manage my workload, I plan and schedule my work in advance, break down large tasks into smaller, manageable steps, and delegate tasks to other team members when appropriate. I also make sure to take breaks and prioritize self-care to ensure that I am able to work effectively and efficiently.

Can you describe a time when you had to handle a problem with a co-worker?

Answer: One time, I had to handle a problem with a co-worker who was not following the bank's procedures for handling customer information. I approached the co-worker and discussed the issue in a professional and respectful manner. I explained the importance of following proper procedures to protect customer information and suggested some changes that could help prevent similar issues in the future. The co-worker was receptive to my feedback and we were able to work together to find a solution. By handling the situation in a positive and collaborative manner, I was able to maintain a good working relationship with my co-worker and help improve the overall operation of the bank.

How do you stay motivated and engaged in your work?

Answer: I stay motivated and engaged in my work by setting personal and professional goals, continually learning and developing my skills, and seeking opportunities to take on new challenges and responsibilities. I also enjoy helping my customers and making a positive impact on their financial lives. I find it fulfilling to work in an industry that can have such a profound and lasting impact on people's lives. Additionally, I stay motivated by working with a supportive and motivated team, and by recognizing and celebrating my accomplishments and successes.

Can you explain how you handle a high volume of customer inquiries or transactions in a busy banking environment?

Answer: In a busy banking environment with a high volume of customer inquiries or transactions, I handle the situation by staying organized and efficient. I prioritize tasks based on urgency and importance and prioritize customer needs. I also use technology, such as automated systems and processes, to help streamline and simplify tasks. When necessary, I work with my team to ensure that we are able to handle the volume of work effectively and efficiently. I also make sure to communicate with customers clearly and professionally, keeping them informed and providing timely responses to their inquiries or requests.

How do you build and maintain positive relationships with customers?

Answer: I build and maintain positive relationships with customers by providing excellent customer service and being responsive to their needs and concerns. I listen actively to their needs and communicate clearly and professionally. I also build trust by following through on commitments, being knowledgeable about the products and services I offer, and providing tailored solutions to meet their unique financial needs. I also seek out opportunities to follow up with customers and check in on their financial wellbeing, demonstrating my commitment to their financial success. By providing a high level of service and building positive, long-term relationships with my customers, I am able to provide the best possible banking experience for them.

Can you explain how you handle challenging customer interactions or complaints?

Answer: When faced with challenging customer interactions or complaints, I handle the situation by staying calm, professional, and empathetic. I listen actively to the customer's concerns and seek to understand their perspective. I then work to resolve the issue in a way that is fair and acceptable to both parties. If necessary, I involve other members of the bank's team or escalate the issue to a higher level of management to ensure a prompt and satisfactory resolution. I also follow up with the customer to ensure that the issue has been resolved to their satisfaction and to reinforce my commitment to providing excellent customer service.

How do you stay up-to-date with changes in the banking industry and regulations?

Answer: To stay up-to-date with changes in the banking industry and regulations, I attend training and continuing education courses, subscribe to industry publications, and actively seek out information from industry experts and thought leaders. I also participate in industry associations and attend conferences and events to network with peers and stay informed about the latest developments in the banking industry. Additionally, I work closely with my bank's compliance and legal departments to ensure that I am aware of any changes in regulations or policies and that I am in compliance with all applicable laws and regulations. By staying informed and engaged with the industry, I am able to provide the best possible service to my customers and help ensure the success of my bank.

How do you ensure the security of sensitive customer information and protect against fraud?

Answer: To ensure the security of sensitive customer information and protect against fraud, I follow the bank's procedures for handling and storing customer information, including using strong passwords and regularly updating them. I also keep customer information confidential and do not share it with unauthorized individuals or entities. In case of suspected fraud or suspicious activity, I report it immediately to the appropriate parties and follow the bank's protocols for investigating and resolving the issue. Additionally, I educate myself and my customers about the latest threats and how to recognize and avoid fraud.

By being vigilant and proactive in protecting customer information and preventing fraud, I am able to help ensure the safety and security of my customers' financial information.

Can you describe a time when you had to make a difficult decision in a banking role?

Answer: One time, I had to make a difficult decision when a customer came to me for a loan, but their credit history indicated that they were a high risk for default. On one hand, I wanted to help the customer, but on the other hand, I was aware that lending money to a high-risk individual could potentially harm the bank's financial stability. After carefully considering all of the factors, I made the difficult decision to decline the loan request. I explained my decision to the customer, provided them with resources for improving their credit, and helped them explore alternative options. Although it was a difficult decision, I was able to maintain my integrity and my commitment to the bank's financial stability while still providing the customer with support and guidance.

How do you handle multiple tasks and priorities while meeting tight deadlines in a fast-paced banking environment?

Answer: In a fast-paced banking environment, I handle multiple tasks and priorities by staying organized and prioritizing tasks based on their level of urgency and importance. I use tools such as task lists and calendars to keep track of my responsibilities and deadlines. I also communicate regularly with my team and seek out their assistance when necessary. When faced with tight deadlines, I prioritize my workload and focus on the most important tasks, using time management strategies such as multitasking and working efficiently.

I also make sure to take breaks when necessary to avoid burnout and maintain my productivity. By staying organized and prioritizing effectively, I am able to meet tight deadlines and successfully manage a heavy workload in a fast-paced banking environment.

How do you handle stressful situations in a banking environment?

Answer: I handle stressful situations in a banking environment by maintaining a professional demeanor, staying calm and focused, and using effective stress-management techniques. I prioritize my workload and break down complex tasks into smaller, more manageable steps. I also take breaks when necessary to clear my mind and recharge. I communicate openly with my team and seek their support when needed. I also practice self-care by engaging in physical activity, eating well, and getting enough sleep. When necessary, I also seek the support of a mental health professional to help me manage my stress. By adopting a holistic approach to stress management, I am able to maintain my well-being and perform at my best in a demanding banking environment.

How do you handle customer complaints in a banking environment?

Answer: I handle customer complaints in a banking environment by listening actively to the customer's concerns, acknowledging their feelings, and taking responsibility for finding a solution. I gather all necessary information to understand the issue and keep the customer informed of the progress and resolution. I work with the customer to find a mutually acceptable solution, apologize if necessary, and follow up to ensure their satisfaction. I also report any recurring issues to the appropriate parties to prevent future occurrences. By being empathetic, responsive, and proactive in addressing customer complaints, I am able to build trust and maintain positive relationships with my customers.

Can you explain the role of technology in modern banking and its impact on customer service?

Answer: Technology plays a critical role in modern banking, as it enables banks to automate many processes and improve efficiency. The use of digital platforms and mobile apps allows customers to access their accounts, transfer funds, and make payments from anywhere, at any time. Technology has also made it easier for banks to process large volumes of transactions, reduce errors, and increase security. However, the increasing reliance on technology has also led to some challenges, such as the need for banks to constantly upgrade their systems and protect against cyber threats. In terms of customer service, technology has enabled banks to provide more personalized and convenient services, such as 24/7 customer support and real-time account updates. However, it has also created a need for banks to invest in customer training and support, to help customers navigate the digital environment and ensure their satisfaction with the services provided.

How do you stay up-to-date with changes in banking regulations and industry developments?

Answer: I stay up-to-date with changes in banking regulations and industry developments by staying informed of the latest news and developments in the banking industry. I regularly read industry publications and attend training sessions and conferences. I also network with colleagues and industry experts to share information and best practices. I also actively seek out opportunities for continuing education and professional development, such as courses and certifications, to deepen my understanding of the banking industry and stay ahead of the curve. By being proactive in my professional development and staying informed, I am able to provide the best possible service to my customers and stay in compliance with banking regulations.

Why do you want to work in the banking industry and what makes you a good fit for this role?

Answer: I am drawn to the banking industry because of its dynamic and challenging nature, as well as its impact on the economy and people's financial well-being. I am a customer-focused individual with strong communication and interpersonal skills, and a deep understanding of banking products and services. I am organized, detail-oriented, and able to work well under pressure, making me well-suited to handle the demands of a fast-paced banking environment. I am also committed to continuous learning and professional development, and am eager to grow my career in the banking industry.

I believe that my combination of skills, experience, and passion for the banking industry make me an excellent fit for a role in this field.

Can you describe a time when you had to make a difficult decision in a banking situation?

Answer: I recall a time when a customer came to me with a request for a loan that was outside of the bank's lending guidelines. The customer was a small business owner who had fallen on hard times and needed the loan to keep his business afloat. After carefully reviewing the customer's financial information and discussing the situation with my supervisor, I made the difficult decision to decline the loan request. I fully explained the bank's lending policies and offered alternative solutions, such as working with a local non-profit organization that specialized in supporting small businesses.

Although the customer was disappointed, they appreciated my honesty and professionalism, and we were able to maintain a positive relationship. I learned that making difficult decisions is a part of my role as a banking professional, and that it is important to communicate openly and effectively with customers to minimize any negative impact.

What do you think sets a successful banking professional apart from others in the industry?

Answer: I believe that a successful banking professional is one who possesses a combination of technical skills, interpersonal skills, and a deep understanding of the industry. They have a strong work ethic, are able to work well under pressure, and are able to handle complex financial transactions with accuracy and efficiency. They are also customer-focused and able to build strong relationships with their customers, based on trust and integrity. Successful banking professionals are proactive in their approach to work, continuously seeking opportunities to improve their skills and knowledge, and are committed to providing the highest level of customer service. They are also knowledgeable about banking regulations and industry developments, and are able to use their expertise to make informed decisions that benefit both the bank and its customers.

How do you handle stressful situations in a banking environment?

Answer: I handle stressful situations in a banking environment by staying calm and composed. I take a step back and assess the situation objectively, and prioritize the tasks that need to be completed. I also communicate effectively with my colleagues and supervisors to ensure that everyone is on the same page and working towards a common goal. I am able to handle multiple tasks simultaneously and remain focused on the task at hand. I also make sure to take breaks when needed and practice self-care to maintain a positive and productive work environment. By using these techniques, I am able to effectively manage stress and maintain a high level of performance in a fast-paced banking environment.

Can you describe a time when you went above and beyond for a customer in a banking situation?

Answer: I recall a time when a customer came to the bank to deposit a large sum of money, but was having difficulty accessing their account due to technical issues. I took the time to listen to the customer's concerns and used my technical skills to resolve the issue. I was able to retrieve the customer's account information and successfully deposit the money. The customer was extremely grateful and impressed by my quick action and exceptional customer service.

I also took the time to follow up with the customer to ensure that their account was functioning properly and that they were satisfied with their banking experience. I believe that going above and beyond for a customer is an important part of my role as a banking professional, and I am committed to providing the highest level of customer service to all of my customers.

How do you stay organized and manage your time effectively in a banking environment?

Answer: I stay organized and manage my time effectively by prioritizing tasks and setting achievable goals for the day. I use a combination of physical and digital tools, such as a to-do list and a calendar, to track my progress and ensure that I am on schedule. I also delegate tasks when appropriate and communicate effectively with my colleagues to avoid duplicating efforts. I am able to multitask efficiently and make the most of my time by focusing on the most important tasks first.

I also make sure to take breaks when needed to avoid burnout and maintain a positive and productive work environment. By using these time management techniques, I am able to effectively balance my workload and provide the highest level of customer service to my customers.

Can you tell us about a time when you had to handle a difficult customer in a banking situation?

Answer: I recall a time when a customer came into the bank with a complaint about a recent transaction. The customer was upset and raised their voice, making it difficult to understand their concerns. I remained calm and listened attentively to their concerns. I then took the time to research the situation and provide a clear and concise explanation of the transaction. I also apologized for any inconvenience the customer may have experienced and offered a solution to resolve the issue. By handling the situation professionally and empathetically, I was able to turn a potentially negative experience into a positive one. The customer left the bank satisfied with my response and the bank's handling of the situation. I believe that being able to handle difficult customers is an important part of my role as a banking professional and requires a combination of empathy, patience, and technical expertise.

How do you stay up-to-date with industry changes and regulatory updates in the banking sector?

Answer: I stay up-to-date with industry changes and regulatory updates in the banking sector by staying informed and continuing my education. I attend industry conferences and workshops to learn about the latest developments and network with other professionals in the field. I also read trade publications and follow relevant organizations and thought leaders on social media to stay informed about new developments. I also have regular training and development opportunities within my organization to ensure that I am up-to-date on the latest regulations and industry best practices.

By staying informed and continuing my education, I am able to provide the highest level of customer service and support the success of my organization.

Can you describe a time when you had to make a difficult decision in a banking situation?

Answer: I recall a time when a customer came to the bank requesting a loan that was outside of their approved credit limit. I was faced with the difficult decision of either denying the loan and potentially losing the customer or approving the loan and potentially putting the bank at risk. After evaluating the customer's financial information and considering their relationship with the bank, I made the difficult decision to deny the loan. I explained the reasons for my decision and offered alternative options for the customer.

Although the customer was initially upset, they appreciated my honesty and professionalism. I believe that making difficult decisions is a critical part of my role as a banking professional and requires a combination of financial acumen, risk management skills, and strong customer service skills.

How do you approach cross-selling bank products and services to customers?

Answer: I approach cross-selling bank products and services to customers by first understanding their financial needs and goals. I listen to the customer's needs and gather information about their financial situation. Based on this information, I then make recommendations for products and services that align with their financial goals and can benefit them. I always prioritize the customer's needs over sales goals and ensure that any product or service I recommend is in the customer's best interest. I also educate the customer about the features and benefits of the products and services, and explain how they can help them achieve their financial goals.

I believe that cross-selling bank products and services should always be customer-focused and not sales-driven.

Can you describe a time when you exceeded expectations in a banking role?

Answer: I recall a time when a customer came into the bank with a complex financial issue that they had been struggling with for months. I took the time to fully understand their situation and offered a tailored solution to their financial problem. The customer was so grateful for my help and was able to finally achieve their financial goals. The customer was so impressed with my service that they became a loyal customer and referred many of their friends and family to the bank. This experience exceeded expectations because I was able to help a customer with a difficult financial situation and turn it into a positive experience for them.

I believe that exceeding expectations is a critical part of my role as a banking professional and requires a combination of technical expertise, customer focus, and a commitment to providing the best possible service.

How do you prioritize your workload and manage multiple tasks effectively in a fast-paced banking environment?

Answer: I prioritize my workload by first identifying the most pressing and time-sensitive tasks and addressing those first. I use various time management techniques, such as prioritizing my to-do list, breaking large projects into smaller tasks, and delegating when necessary. I also utilize technology, such as project management software and calendars, to help me stay organized and on track. In a fast-paced banking environment, it's essential to be flexible and adapt to changing priorities as they arise. I maintain a positive attitude and remain calm under pressure, which helps me to effectively manage multiple tasks and prioritize my workload.

Can you explain how you maintain confidentiality and security when handling sensitive information in a banking role?

Answer: I maintain confidentiality and security when handling sensitive information by following the bank's established policies and procedures, such as password protection, encryption, and secure data storage. I am also trained in data privacy laws and regulations and understand the importance of protecting sensitive information. I only access customer information that is necessary for me to perform my job, and I never share confidential information with unauthorized parties. Additionally, I ensure that all paper and electronic records are stored securely and disposed of appropriately.

I understand that maintaining the confidentiality and security of sensitive information is a critical part of my role as a banking professional, and I take this responsibility seriously.

How do you handle difficult customers or clients in a banking setting?

Answer: I handle difficult customers or clients in a banking setting by remaining calm, professional, and empathetic. I listen actively to the customer's concerns and try to understand their perspective. I then address their concerns by providing clear and concise information, and I offer a solution to the issue at hand. I apologize if the customer is unhappy, and I do my best to make the situation right. I believe that treating every customer with respect and understanding is key to resolving difficult situations. Additionally, I seek to turn a negative situation into a positive experience by providing excellent customer service and demonstrating a commitment to customer satisfaction.

I believe that every customer interaction provides an opportunity to build customer trust and loyalty.

How do you stay up-to-date on the latest banking products and services, industry trends, and regulations?

Answer: I stay up-to-date on the latest banking products and services, industry trends, and regulations by attending industry conferences, participating in training sessions and workshops, and reading industry publications. I also network with colleagues and attend industry events to stay informed about the latest developments in the banking industry. I believe that ongoing education and professional development are critical to maintaining my expertise and providing the highest level of customer service. Additionally, I keep abreast of changes in regulations and ensure that I follow all relevant laws and guidelines in my banking role. Staying up-to-date on the latest industry trends and regulations allows me to provide the best possible advice and solutions to my customers.

Can you describe a time when you went above and beyond for a customer in a banking role?

Answer: I recall a time when a customer came to me with a problem regarding their account. They were upset and frustrated, and I could sense that they were at their wits' end. I listened actively to their concerns and spent extra time researching their account to find a solution. I was able to resolve the issue by working with the customer and various internal departments, and I even went as far as to arrange for additional follow-up to ensure that the customer was satisfied. The customer was so grateful for my extra efforts, and they expressed their appreciation by writing a positive review of their experience.

I felt proud to have been able to turn a potentially negative experience into a positive one, and I believe that this demonstrates my commitment to providing excellent customer service in a banking setting.

Can you discuss your experience with cross-selling and up-selling banking products and services?

Answer: I have experience with cross-selling and up-selling banking products and services by identifying customer needs and offering tailored solutions. I take the time to understand my customers' financial goals and needs, and I make recommendations for products and services that can help them achieve their objectives. I also stay up-to-date on the latest banking products and services, so I can provide my customers with the most relevant and current information. I believe that cross-selling and up-selling are important for building customer relationships, and I approach these activities with a customer-focused mindset. My goal is always to provide value to the customer and enhance their overall banking experience.

Can you discuss your experience with loan processing and underwriting?

Answer: I have experience with loan processing and underwriting, including gathering and verifying customer information, evaluating loan applications, and making credit decisions. I am familiar with loan underwriting guidelines and regulations, and I ensure that all loan applications are processed in a timely and accurate manner. I have a strong attention to detail, and I take great care in reviewing loan applications to ensure that all necessary information is included and that the customer's creditworthiness is accurately assessed. I work closely with customers to gather all necessary information and ensure that their loan application is processed efficiently and effectively. I believe that my experience with loan processing and underwriting makes me well-suited for a banking role, as I am able to provide high-quality service and support to customers in their loan needs.

How do you handle confidential information in a banking setting?

Answer: I handle confidential information in a banking setting with the utmost care and attention to security. I am familiar with the various privacy laws and regulations that govern banking, and I take steps to ensure that customer information is kept confidential at all times. I never share customer information without their permission, and I follow strict security protocols when accessing or handling confidential information. I believe that trust is key to building strong customer relationships, and I take great care to protect my customers' confidential information. I also stay informed about the latest security trends and techniques, and I take a proactive approach to ensuring that customer information is protected against potential security threats.

Can you discuss your experience with risk management in a banking setting?

Answer: I have experience with risk management in a banking setting, including assessing and managing credit risk, market risk, and operational risk. I have a strong understanding of the various risks associated with banking, and I work closely with the risk management team to ensure that risks are effectively identified and managed. I use data analysis and other tools to evaluate risk and make informed decisions, and I stay informed about the latest risk management techniques and trends. I believe that a proactive approach to risk management is critical to maintaining the health and stability of a financial institution, and I take a customer-focused approach to ensuring that customer assets are protected and that the bank is operating in a safe and secure manner.

Can you explain the importance of customer service in banking?

Answer: Customer service is extremely important in banking as it is a key factor in building and maintaining customer relationships. Providing high-quality customer service is essential in creating a positive customer experience, and it helps to establish trust and confidence in the bank. Good customer service involves listening to customer needs and concerns, providing accurate and timely information, and resolving any issues or problems in a professional and efficient manner. A focus on customer service can also lead to increased customer loyalty and repeat business, as well as positive word-of-mouth referrals. In a competitive banking industry, providing exceptional customer service is crucial in standing out from the competition and building a strong reputation.

Can you describe a difficult customer interaction you have had and how you handled it?

Answer: I once had a difficult customer interaction where a customer was frustrated with the bank's policies and procedures, and he became very upset and raised his voice. I listened to the customer's concerns, calmly addressed each issue, and offered possible solutions. I showed empathy and understanding towards the customer's situation, and I was patient and professional in my approach. I was able to resolve the issue to the customer's satisfaction and he left the branch feeling satisfied with the outcome.

I believe that good customer service requires a patient and empathetic approach, and that it is important to remain calm and professional in even the most difficult of customer interactions.

How do you stay organized and manage your time effectively in a fast-paced banking environment?

Answer: I stay organized and manage my time effectively by prioritizing my tasks and breaking them down into smaller, manageable parts. I use various tools such as a task list, calendars, and reminders to keep track of my responsibilities and deadlines. I also communicate regularly with my colleagues and superiors to ensure that everyone is on the same page, and I am proactive in seeking assistance when needed. In a fast-paced banking environment, it is also important to be adaptable and flexible, and I am always ready to adjust my priorities as needed. I believe that good time management and organization are critical in providing high-quality customer service, and I make it a priority to use my time and resources effectively in order to deliver the best results.

Can you explain the role of technology in the banking industry?

Answer: Technology plays a vital role in the banking industry, as it helps banks to increase efficiency, improve customer service, and reduce costs. Technology has enabled banks to automate many processes and make banking services more accessible to customers. For example, online banking and mobile banking allow customers to access their accounts and perform transactions from anywhere, at any time. Technology has also made it possible for banks to offer new and innovative products and services, such as digital wallets and mobile payments. Additionally, technology is used to detect and prevent fraud, and to provide customers with greater security and privacy.

The banking industry continues to evolve with advancements in technology, and it is important for banks to keep up with the latest developments in order to remain competitive.

How do you keep up-to-date with the latest developments in the banking industry?

Answer: To stay up-to-date with the latest developments in the banking industry, I regularly read trade publications, attend industry conferences and events, and participate in training and professional development opportunities. I also network with my colleagues and other professionals in the industry to share ideas and insights, and I actively seek out new and innovative solutions that can improve my knowledge and skills. Additionally, I stay informed about new laws and regulations that impact the banking industry, and I make it a point to stay current with the latest technologies and trends in banking. I believe that continuous learning and professional development are critical in today's rapidly changing banking industry, and I make it a priority to stay ahead of the curve.

How do you handle difficult customer situations in a bank?

Answer: When handling difficult customer situations, my approach is to remain calm, professional, and empathetic. I listen to the customer's concerns and try to understand their perspective. I then provide clear, concise, and accurate information to address their issues and find a solution that meets their needs. If a customer is dissatisfied, I apologize and take responsibility for the situation, and I work to find a resolution that is in the best interest of both the customer and the bank. If a resolution cannot be reached, I escalate the issue to a higher authority for further assistance.

I believe that clear and open communication, as well as a commitment to finding a mutually acceptable solution, are key to handling difficult customer situations in a bank.

How do you ensure the security and privacy of customer information in a bank?

Answer: Ensuring the security and privacy of customer information is a top priority in a bank. To achieve this, I follow all relevant laws and regulations, such as the Gramm-Leach-Bliley Act and the Bank Secrecy Act. I also implement internal policies and procedures to protect customer information, such as using strong passwords, regularly updating security software, and securely storing and disposing of confidential information. I also educate customers on best practices for protecting their personal information and inform them of the bank's security measures.

Additionally, I report any potential security incidents to the appropriate authorities and follow established procedures for responding to such incidents. By consistently following these measures, I can help ensure the security and privacy of customer information in a bank.

Can you explain the concept of asset liability management in banking?

Answer: Asset liability management (ALM) is a key concept in banking that refers to the management of a bank's assets and liabilities to ensure that the bank has sufficient liquidity and capital to meet its obligations and maintain stability in times of economic stress. ALM involves balancing the bank's assets, such as loans and investments, with its liabilities, such as deposits and borrowings, to manage risk and optimize returns. This includes managing the bank's interest rate risk, credit risk, and liquidity risk. The goal of ALM is to minimize the bank's exposure to market and financial risks, and to ensure that the bank can meet its obligations to customers, regulators, and other stakeholders. ALM is a critical function in banking and requires careful monitoring and analysis to ensure that the bank operates in a safe and sound manner.

Can you explain the role of the Federal Reserve System in the banking industry?

Answer: The Federal Reserve System, also known as the Fed, is the central bank of the United States and is responsible for implementing monetary policy, supervising and regulating banks, and maintaining the stability of the financial system. The Fed works to achieve its objectives by influencing the money supply, interest rates, and credit conditions in the economy. It also provides financial services to the U.S. government and acts as a lender of last resort in times of financial stress.

The Fed's role in the banking industry is important, as it helps to ensure the stability and safety of the financial system, which benefits both banks and their customers. By supervising and regulating banks, the Fed helps to prevent and mitigate financial risks, and by implementing monetary policy, it helps to promote economic growth and stability.

Can you explain the difference between a commercial bank and an investment bank?

Answer: Commercial banks and investment banks serve different functions in the financial system. Commercial banks are financial institutions that accept deposits from individuals and businesses and make loans to those same customers. They focus on traditional banking activities such as checking and savings accounts, loans, mortgages, and credit cards. Commercial banks play an important role in the economy by providing a safe place for individuals and businesses to store their money and by financing the investments and activities of the real economy.

Investment banks, on the other hand, are financial institutions that specialize in underwriting, issuing, and trading securities, as well as providing financial advice and risk management services to corporations, governments, and other institutions. Investment banks typically do not accept deposits from the public and do not provide traditional banking services. Instead, they focus on complex financial activities such as mergers and acquisitions, debt and equity financing, and securities trading.

In summary, the main difference between commercial banks and investment banks is their focus and the type of services they provide. Commercial banks focus on traditional banking activities and provide services to individual and business customers, while investment banks focus on complex financial activities and provide services to corporations, governments, and other institutions.

What is Basel III and what is its purpose?

Answer: Basel III is a set of international banking regulations that were developed by the Basel Committee on Banking Supervision (BCBS) in response to the financial crisis of 2008. The regulations were designed to strengthen the global banking system by improving the quality and quantity of capital held by banks, enhancing their risk management practices, and improving their overall stability and resilience. The key components of Basel III include:

- Higher capital requirements: Banks are required to hold more and higher-quality capital to reduce their exposure to risk.
- Liquidity standards: Banks must maintain sufficient liquidity to meet their obligations in times of stress.
- Improved risk management: Banks must implement stronger risk management practices, such as stress testing, to identify and manage potential risks.
- Enhanced disclosure and transparency: Banks must provide more information to regulators and the public about their financial condition and risk exposure.

The overall goal of Basel III is to create a safer and more resilient banking system that is better equipped to handle financial stress and prevent future crises. By improving the quality and quantity of capital held by banks, enhancing their risk management practices, and increasing their overall stability and resilience, Basel III aims to promote financial stability and protect depositors and taxpayers.

Can you explain the role of the Federal Reserve (the Fed) in the US banking system?

Answer: The Federal Reserve, commonly referred to as the Fed, is the central bank of the United States. It was created in 1913 with the aim of providing the US economy with a stable and flexible monetary and financial system. The Fed plays a critical role in the US banking system by performing several key functions, including:

- Monetary policy: The Fed sets monetary policy by controlling the supply of money and credit in the economy. This helps to influence interest rates, inflation, and overall economic activity.
- Supervision and regulation: The Fed is responsible for supervising and regulating banks and other financial institutions to ensure that they operate safely and soundly, and in compliance with laws and regulations.
- Financial stability: The Fed plays an important role in promoting stability in the financial system by working to prevent and resolve financial crises.
- Payment system: The Fed operates the payment system, which enables banks and other financial institutions to settle their transactions electronically.
- Reserve bank: The Fed acts as a "banker's bank" by holding the reserves of commercial banks and providing them with loans and other financial services.

In summary, the Fed plays a critical role in the US banking system by performing several key functions that help to promote stability, ensure the safety and soundness of banks, and support the overall health of the economy.

Can you explain the difference between a savings account and a checking account?

Answer: A savings account and a checking account are both types of deposit accounts offered by banks, but they are designed for different purposes.

- A savings account is designed for individuals to save and earn interest on their deposits. Savings accounts typically offer a lower interest rate compared to other types of accounts and have a limited number of transactions allowed per month, as the focus is on saving money and earning interest, not everyday spending.
- A checking account, on the other hand, is designed for everyday spending and transactions. Checking accounts offer the convenience of being able to write checks, make debit card purchases, and access money through ATMs. Checking accounts typically do not earn interest and may have monthly maintenance fees.

In summary, savings accounts are best for individuals who want to save money and earn interest, while checking accounts are best for individuals who want a convenient way to manage their daily transactions.

Can you explain the difference between a fixed deposit and a recurring deposit?

Answer: Fixed deposit (FD) and recurring deposit (RD) are two types of deposit accounts offered by banks, but they are designed for different purposes.

- A fixed deposit is a type of deposit account where an individual can deposit a lump sum amount for a fixed period of time, usually ranging from one to ten years. The interest rate on a fixed deposit is generally higher than a savings account and is fixed for the entire term of the deposit. At the end of the fixed deposit term, the individual receives the original deposit amount plus the accumulated interest.
- A recurring deposit, on the other hand, is a type of deposit account where an individual can deposit a fixed amount of money on a regular basis, usually every month. The interest rate on a recurring deposit is also generally higher than a savings

account and is fixed for the entire term of the deposit. At the end of the recurring deposit term, the individual receives the accumulated deposit amount plus the accumulated interest.

In summary, fixed deposit is best for individuals who have a lump sum amount and want to earn a higher interest rate, while recurring deposit is best for individuals who have a regular source of income and want to save a fixed amount of money every month.

Can you explain the difference between a credit card and a debit card?

Answer: A credit card and a debit card are both types of payment cards, but they work in different ways.

- A credit card is a type of loan that allows individuals to make purchases and withdraw cash advances, up to a predetermined credit limit. When an individual uses a credit card, they are borrowing money from the issuer and are required to repay the borrowed amount, plus interest and other fees, at a later date.
- A debit card, on the other hand, is linked to an individual's checking account and allows them to make purchases and withdraw cash by directly accessing their checking account funds. When an individual uses a debit card, the funds are immediately deducted from their checking account balance.

In summary, credit cards offer the ability to borrow money, but also come with higher fees and interest rates. Debit cards offer the convenience of using plastic, but are limited to the amount of funds in the linked checking account.

Can you explain what an equity share is?

Answer: Equity share, also known as common stock or simply stock, is a type of security that represents ownership in a company. When an individual buys an equity share in a company, they become a shareholder and own a small part of the company. Equity shareholders are entitled to a share of the company's profits and have a claim on the company's assets in the event of liquidation.

Equity shares are also a source of capital for companies, as they can issue new shares to raise funds for growth and expansion. The price of equity shares is determined by supply and demand in the stock market, and can fluctuate based on the financial performance of the company, overall market conditions, and other factors.

In summary, equity shares represent a form of ownership in a company and offer the potential for capital appreciation and a share of company profits. However, they also carry risk, as the value of the shares can decrease if the company performs poorly.

Can you explain the difference between a savings account and a current account?

Answer: A savings account and a current account are both types of deposit accounts offered by banks, but they are designed for different purposes.

- A savings account is a type of deposit account that pays interest on the funds deposited. Savings accounts are typically used by individuals to save money and earn a return on their savings. They often have restrictions on the number of transactions that can be made, and may have higher interest rates compared to other types of deposit accounts.
- A current account, on the other hand, is designed for individuals or businesses that have a high volume of transactions. Current accounts do not usually pay interest on the funds deposited, but offer a range of other services such as overdraft facilities and check writing.

In summary, savings accounts are designed for individuals looking to save money and earn a return, while current accounts are designed for individuals or businesses with high transaction volumes.

Can you explain the role of the Central Bank in a country's economy?

Answer: The Central Bank of a country plays a crucial role in the country's economy by acting as a regulator, supervisor, and lender of last resort. The main responsibilities of the Central Bank include:

- Monetary policy: The Central Bank sets monetary policy, including interest rates, to control the supply of money in the economy and maintain price stability.
- Regulator and supervisor of the banking system: The Central Bank is responsible for supervising and regulating the banking system to ensure the stability and integrity of the financial system.
- Lender of last resort: The Central Bank acts as a lender of last resort, providing emergency loans to banks and financial institutions in times of financial crisis.
- Currency issuer: The Central Bank is responsible for issuing and managing the country's currency, including the issuance of new notes and coins.

In summary, the Central Bank plays a vital role in maintaining stability in the country's financial system and economy, and is responsible for implementing monetary policy, supervising and regulating the banking system, acting as a lender of last resort, and issuing currency.

Can you explain the difference between a fixed deposit and a recurring deposit?

Answer: Fixed deposits and recurring deposits are both types of savings instruments offered by banks, but they have some key differences.

- Fixed deposits (FDs) are a type of savings instrument where the depositor agrees to keep a certain amount of money with the bank for a fixed period of time. The interest rate offered on fixed deposits is usually higher than that offered on savings accounts and the rate of interest is fixed for the entire tenure of the deposit.
- Recurring deposits (RDs) are similar to fixed deposits, but instead of a lump sum deposit, the depositor makes regular,

equal payments into the account over a specified period of time. The interest rate offered on recurring deposits is usually higher than that offered on savings accounts.

In summary, the main difference between fixed deposits and recurring deposits is that in fixed deposits the deposit is made as a lump sum, while in recurring deposits the deposit is made in smaller, regular instalments. Additionally, the interest rate offered on fixed deposits is generally higher than that offered on recurring deposits.

Can you explain the role of a loan officer in a bank?

Answer: A loan officer is an individual working in a bank who is responsible for evaluating loan applications and deciding whether or not to approve the loan. The main responsibilities of a loan officer include:

- Evaluating loan applications: The loan officer reviews loan applications and assesses the applicant's creditworthiness and ability to repay the loan.
- Determining loan terms: Based on the loan application, the loan officer determines the loan amount, interest rate, repayment period, and any collateral requirements.
- Verifying information: The loan officer verifies the information provided in the loan application, including the applicant's income, employment status, and credit history.
- Approving or denying loan applications: Based on the information gathered during the loan evaluation process, the loan officer either approves or denies the loan application.
- Monitoring loan performance: The loan officer is responsible for monitoring the performance of the loan, including payment history, loan balances, and any potential default issues.

In summary, a loan officer plays a crucial role in the loan application process, evaluating loan applications, determining loan terms, verifying information, approving or denying loan applications, and monitoring loan performance.

What is the purpose of KYC (Know Your Customer) in banking?

Answer: KYC stands for "Know Your Customer" and refers to the process of verifying the identity of a bank's customers. The purpose of KYC in banking is to ensure that banks have accurate and complete information about their customers, and to prevent financial crimes such as money laundering and terrorist financing.

The KYC process typically involves collecting and verifying the customer's personal and financial information, including their name, address, date of birth, and government-issued identification number. Banks may also ask for additional information such as employment details, source of income, and financial history.

By conducting KYC, banks can ensure that they are doing business with legitimate customers and not with individuals or organizations involved in illegal activities. This helps to maintain the integrity of the financial system and protects both the bank and its customers.

In summary, the purpose of KYC in banking is to verify the identity of bank customers, prevent financial crimes, and maintain the integrity of the financial system.

Can you explain the difference between savings account and current account in a bank?

Answer: A savings account and a current account are two different types of bank accounts that serve different purposes.

- A savings account is designed for individuals who want to save money and earn interest on their deposits. Savings accounts typically have lower interest rates and restrictions on the number of transactions that can be made each month. The main purpose of a savings account is to help individuals save money and grow their wealth over time.
- On the other hand, a current account is designed for individuals or businesses who need to make a high volume of transactions on a regular basis. Current accounts do not typically earn interest, but offer more flexible transaction options, including

overdraft facilities, check-writing abilities, and free online banking services. The main purpose of a current account is to provide a convenient and flexible way to manage daily financial transactions.

In summary, the main difference between a savings account and a current account is their intended purpose, with savings accounts designed for saving and earning interest, and current accounts designed for frequent transactions and ease of use.

Can you explain what is the role of the central bank in the banking system?

Answer: The central bank is a key player in the banking system and plays a critical role in maintaining the stability and integrity of the financial system.

The main role of the central bank is to conduct monetary policy and regulate the supply of money in the economy. This involves setting interest rates, controlling the money supply, and managing the exchange rate between the country's currency and other currencies.

In addition to conducting monetary policy, the central bank also acts as a regulator of the banking system. This includes supervising and regulating commercial banks, ensuring they operate in a safe and sound manner, and protecting the interests of depositors. The central bank may also act as a lender of last resort, providing emergency loans to commercial banks in times of financial crisis.

The central bank also plays a role in promoting financial stability, by monitoring and assessing the overall health of the financial system and taking action to prevent or mitigate financial crises.

In summary, the role of the central bank in the banking system is to conduct monetary policy, regulate the banking system, promote financial stability, and act as a lender of last resort in times of financial crisis.

Can you explain the difference between a commercial bank and an investment bank?

Answer: Commercial banks and investment banks are two distinct types of financial institutions that serve different purposes and operate in different ways.

- Commercial banks are financial institutions that primarily engage in accepting deposits and making loans to individuals and businesses. They provide a wide range of financial services to their customers, including checking and savings accounts, mortgages, personal loans, and business loans. Commercial banks also offer services such as wealth management, insurance, and investment advice.
- Investment banks, on the other hand, are financial institutions that specialize in underwriting, issuing, and trading securities, such as stocks and bonds. Investment banks also provide services such as financial advisory and mergers and acquisitions (M&A) services to corporations and governments. Unlike commercial banks, investment banks do not take deposits from the general public and do not make loans.

In summary, commercial banks primarily focus on providing traditional banking services to individuals and businesses, while investment banks specialize in investment banking services such as underwriting, issuing, and trading securities, and providing financial advisory services.

What is the difference between a savings account and a checking account?

Answer: Savings accounts and checking accounts are two different types of bank accounts that serve different purposes.

- A savings account is designed to help individuals save money and earn interest on their deposits. Savings accounts usually have a low interest rate and a limit on the number of monthly transactions. This type of account is meant for individuals who want to save money for long-term goals such as a down payment on a house or for emergency funds.

- A checking account, on the other hand, is designed to provide individuals with easy access to their funds for everyday transactions such as paying bills, making purchases, and writing checks. Checking accounts usually do not earn interest and may have fees, such as monthly maintenance fees or transaction fees.

In summary, savings accounts are meant for saving and earning interest, while checking accounts are meant for everyday transactions. Individuals should choose the type of account that best suits their financial needs.

What is the Federal Reserve System and what is its role in the U.S. economy?

Answer: The Federal Reserve System, also known as the Fed, is the central banking system of the United States. It was established in 1913 by the Federal Reserve Act and is responsible for implementing monetary policy and regulating banks.

The Fed has several key responsibilities in the U.S. economy, including:

- Conducting monetary policy: The Fed sets interest rates and implements monetary policy to influence the supply of money and credit in the economy. This helps to maintain price stability and promote maximum employment.
- Regulating banks: The Fed is responsible for supervising and regulating banks to ensure the stability and safety of the banking system.
- Maintaining stability in the financial system: The Fed serves as a lender of last resort during times of financial crisis, providing liquidity to banks and other financial institutions to help stabilize the financial system.
- Processing and clearing payments: The Fed processes and clears payments between banks, such as checks, electronic transfers, and wire transfers.

In summary, the Fed plays a critical role in maintaining the stability and health of the U.S. economy through its responsibilities in conducting monetary policy, regulating banks, maintaining stability in the financial system, and processing and clearing payments.

Can you explain the difference between a traditional bank and an online bank?

Answer: A traditional bank is a physical bank that operates through brick-and-mortar branches, where customers can visit in person to conduct transactions, such as depositing checks or withdrawing cash. They also offer a wide range of financial products and services, including loans, mortgages, and investment services.

On the other hand, an online bank is a bank that operates primarily through the internet. Customers can access their accounts and conduct transactions online, without the need to visit a physical branch. Online banks often have lower overhead costs than traditional banks, allowing them to offer higher interest rates on deposits and lower fees. However, they may have limited services compared to traditional banks.

In summary, the main difference between traditional banks and online banks is the way they deliver their services. Traditional banks offer a full range of services through physical branches, while online banks offer a more limited range of services primarily through the internet.

How do you ensure the security of online banking transactions?

Answer: Ensuring the security of online banking transactions is a top priority for financial institutions. There are several measures that banks take to ensure the security of online transactions, including:

- Encryption: Banks use secure encryption technology to protect sensitive information during online transactions. This helps to ensure that the information cannot be intercepted or accessed by unauthorized individuals.

- Two-factor authentication: Banks may require customers to enter a password and a unique code sent to their phone or email before they can access their accounts online. This helps to prevent unauthorized access to accounts.
- Firewalls and anti-virus software: Banks use firewalls and anti-virus software to protect their systems from potential cyber attacks.
- Monitoring and detection systems: Banks use systems to monitor and detect any suspicious activity on their networks, such as unusual login patterns or large transactions.
- Customer education: Banks educate their customers on best practices for online banking security, such as using strong passwords and avoiding phishing scams.

By implementing these and other security measures, banks help to ensure the security of online banking transactions for their customers.

What is your understanding of the regulatory environment in the banking industry?

Answer: The regulatory environment in the banking industry is a complex and ever-changing landscape. The banking sector is heavily regulated by various government agencies, such as the Federal Reserve System, the Office of the Comptroller of the Currency, and the Federal Deposit Insurance Corporation. These agencies have a broad range of responsibilities, including setting standards for bank operations, supervising bank activities, and ensuring the stability of the financial system.

In addition to these federal agencies, there are also state-level regulators who oversee banking activities in their respective states. The regulations in the banking industry are designed to protect consumers, ensure the stability of the financial system, and promote fair competition in the industry.

It is important for banking professionals to have a strong understanding of the regulatory environment in order to ensure compliance with laws and regulations and to minimize the risk of legal or financial penalties. This requires staying up-to-date with changes in the regulatory landscape and having a thorough understanding of the regulations and how they apply to specific banking activities.

How would you describe your approach to risk management in banking?

Answer: Effective risk management is critical in the banking industry. In my approach to risk management, I always prioritize the identification and assessment of potential risks. This involves regularly reviewing and updating our risk management strategies, policies and procedures.

I believe in maintaining a balanced approach to risk management, where I take into account the potential impact of risks on our organization, as well as the potential benefits of taking certain risks. I also believe in involving all relevant stakeholders in the risk management process, including senior management, risk management staff, and business unit managers.

I also place a strong emphasis on developing a culture of risk management within the organization. This involves educating employees on the importance of risk management, and encouraging them to identify and report potential risks.

In addition, I believe in regularly monitoring and reviewing the effectiveness of our risk management strategies and making adjustments as needed. By continuously improving our risk management processes, I believe we can minimize the impact of risks on our organization and ultimately ensure long-term success.

What are the steps involved in loan processing?

Answer: The steps involved in loan processing typically include:

- Customer application: The first step involves the customer filling out a loan application and submitting the required documentation.
- Credit check: The bank then performs a credit check on the customer to assess their creditworthiness.

- Verification of information: The bank verifies the information provided by the customer and checks their employment, income, and other financial details.
- Approval/rejection: Based on the credit check and verification of information, the bank decides whether to approve or reject the loan application.
- Loan documentation: If the loan is approved, the bank prepares the loan agreement and other necessary documents for the customer to sign.
- Disbursement: The loan amount is then disbursed to the customer, either directly or through a third party.
- Repayment: The customer begins repaying the loan as per the agreed repayment schedule.

It's important to note that the exact steps involved in loan processing may vary from bank to bank and may also depend on the type of loan being processed. However, the above steps give a general overview of the loan processing process.

What is the difference between a savings account and a checking account?

Answer: A savings account and a checking account are two different types of bank accounts that are used for different purposes.

A savings account is typically used to save money and earn interest. It usually has a lower interest rate and is meant for customers who want to save money over a longer period of time.

A checking account, on the other hand, is meant for daily transactions and is designed for customers who want to easily access their funds for expenses such as rent, bills, or purchases. Checking accounts usually have no or very low interest rates and offer customers the ability to write checks or use a debit card to withdraw money from an ATM.

In summary, a savings account is ideal for saving and earning interest, while a checking account is ideal for daily transactions and easy access to funds.

What is the purpose of a credit report?

Answer: A credit report is a detailed summary of an individual's credit history, which includes information about their borrowing and repayment habits. The purpose of a credit report is to provide lenders, landlords, and other organizations with information about a person's creditworthiness and ability to repay debt.

A credit report will typically include information about an individual's credit card balances, loan amounts, payment history, and any late payments or collections. This information is used by lenders and other organizations to evaluate the risk of lending money or offering credit to an individual.

Having a good credit report is important because it can affect an individual's ability to get approved for loans, credit cards, and even rental applications. It is also used to determine the interest rate and terms of a loan or credit card.

What is the difference between a savings account and a checking account?

Answer: A savings account is designed to help individuals save money and earn interest on their deposits. It typically pays a higher interest rate compared to a checking account, but also has more restrictions, such as limited transactions and withdrawal amounts.

A checking account is intended for everyday transactions, such as paying bills and making purchases. It is more accessible than a savings account and usually offers unlimited transactions and check-writing capabilities. However, interest rates on checking accounts are generally lower than those offered on savings accounts.

In general, a savings account is best for individuals looking to grow their savings and earn interest, while a checking account is better for those who need frequent access to their money for day-to-day transactions.

What is the role of a bank in the economy?

Answer: Banks play a critical role in the economy by providing a range of financial services and products to individuals, businesses, and governments. These services include accepting deposits, issuing loans, and providing a range of investment and payment services.

Banks also play a crucial role in facilitating the flow of funds in the economy. They help to move funds from savers to borrowers, which helps to stimulate economic growth and development. They also help to regulate the money supply by controlling the amount of credit available in the market.

In addition, banks serve as intermediaries in financial markets by connecting borrowers with lenders, and by pooling funds from depositors to provide capital for investment opportunities.

Overall, the role of banks in the economy is to provide financial stability, facilitate economic growth, and promote access to credit and financial services.

CHAPTER FIVE

General Questions and answers

What is the role of a Credit Officer in a bank?

A: A Credit Officer is responsible for evaluating loan applications, conducting credit checks, determining creditworthiness of applicants, and making lending decisions based on their findings. They are also responsible for managing existing loan accounts and ensuring timely repayment of loans.

What is a Non-performing Loan (NPL)?

A: A Non-performing Loan (NPL) is a loan where the borrower has failed to make regular payments for a specified period of time. NPLs have a negative impact on the financial health of a bank, as they are unlikely to be fully repaid and can result in a loss for the bank.

How does a bank manage its risk exposure?

A: Banks use a variety of risk management techniques to minimize their exposure to financial, operational, and market risks. These techniques include diversifying their portfolio, setting aside reserves, using hedging strategies, and implementing risk management systems and processes. Banks also regularly monitor and review their risk exposure to ensure that it remains within acceptable limits.

What is the role of the Reserve Bank of India (RBI)?

A: The Reserve Bank of India (RBI) is the central bank of India and is responsible for managing the country's monetary policy and regulation of the banking sector. It is also responsible for maintaining financial stability, issuing currency, managing foreign exchange reserves, and promoting a sound banking system. The RBI also acts as the regulator of the Indian banking sector and ensures that banks comply with regulatory requirements and standards.

What is an EFT?

EFT stands for Electronic Funds Transfer, which refers to the transfer of funds from one bank account to another, without the use of paper checks or cash.

What is an overdraft fee?

An overdraft fee is a fee charged by a bank when a checking account balance goes below zero and the bank covers the overdraft by paying the overdraft transaction.

What is compound interest?

Compound interest is the interest calculated on the original principal and also on the accumulated interest of previous periods.

How is compound interest calculated?

Compound interest is calculated using the formula: $A = P (1 + r/n)^{(nt)}$, where A is the total amount after t years, P is the principal amount, r is the interest rate, n is the number of times interest is compounded per year, and t is the number of years.

What is an interest rate?

An interest rate is the percentage of an amount of money charged by a lender to a borrower for the use of money.

What is an APR (Annual Percentage Rate)?

An APR (Annual Percentage Rate) is the total cost of borrowing money, expressed as a yearly rate, including both the interest rate and any fees.

How is interest calculated on a loan?

Interest on a loan is calculated by multiplying the interest rate by the loan balance.

What is a mortgage?

A mortgage is a loan used to purchase a property, typically with a long repayment period and a fixed or adjustable interest rate.

What is a loan amortization schedule?

A loan amortization schedule is a table that shows the payment schedule, including the amount of principal and interest paid in each payment, for a loan over its life.

How is loan amortization calculated?

Loan amortization is calculated by dividing the loan amount by the number of payments to be made, which determines the amount of each payment. The payments are then applied to both principal and interest, with the balance of the loan decreasing over time.

What is a savings account interest rate?

A savings account interest rate is the rate at which a bank pays interest on the balance in a savings account.

How is the interest rate on a savings account determined?

The interest rate on a savings account is determined by the Federal Reserve's monetary policy and competition among banks for customers.

What is a certificate of deposit (CD)?

A certificate of deposit (CD) is a type of savings account that pays a fixed rate of interest for a specified period of time, typically ranging from a few months to several years.

How is the interest rate on a CD determined?

The interest rate on a CD is determined by market conditions and the issuing bank's funding costs.

What is a savings account?

A savings account is a type of bank account where funds are deposited and earn interest, and typically allow for limited withdrawals and deposits.

What is a checking account?

A checking account is a type of bank account that allows for frequent transactions, such as deposits and withdrawals, and is typically used for daily expenses.

What is an overdraft fee?

An overdraft fee is a fee charged by a bank when the account holder withdraws more funds than are available in the account.

What is a minimum balance requirement for a bank account?

A minimum balance requirement is the minimum amount of money that a bank requires an account holder to maintain in an account in order to avoid fees.

What is a credit score?

A credit score is a numerical representation of an individual's creditworthiness, based on a range of factors including payment history, credit utilization, length of credit history, and types of credit.

How is a credit score calculated?

A credit score is calculated using algorithms that take into account a range of factors, including payment history, credit utilization, length of credit history, and types of credit. The exact method of calculation varies among credit reporting agencies.

What is a credit report?

A credit report is a record of an individual's credit history, including information on credit accounts, payment history, and outstanding debts.

How often is a credit report updated?

A credit report is typically updated every month, and new information is added as it is reported to the credit reporting agencies by lenders.

What is a credit utilization rate?

A credit utilization rate is the percentage of credit available on a credit account that is currently being used.

How does a high credit utilization rate affect a credit score?

A high credit utilization rate can negatively affect a credit score because it indicates to lenders that the individual may be overextended and may be at a higher risk for default.

What is a loan default?

A loan default is when a borrower fails to repay a loan according to the terms agreed upon in the loan agreement.

What is a collateral?

Collateral is property or other assets that a borrower puts up as security for a loan, to be used to repay the loan if the borrower fails to do so.

What is a personal loan?

A personal loan is an unsecured loan, meaning it is not backed by collateral, that can be used for a variety of purposes, such as consolidating debt or making a large purchase.

What is a secured loan?

A secured loan is a loan that is backed by collateral, such as a house or a car, which the lender can seize if the borrower fails to repay the loan according to the terms agreed upon in the loan agreement.

What is an unsecured loan?

An unsecured loan is a loan that is not backed by collateral and is based on the borrower's creditworthiness and ability to repay the loan.

What is a line of credit?

A line of credit is a loan in which the borrower can access funds up to a certain limit, as needed, and only pay interest on the funds that are actually used.

What is a credit card?

A credit card is a type of loan in which the borrower can access funds up to a certain limit, and is required to repay the loan with interest.

What is a balance transfer credit card?

A balance transfer credit card is a credit card that allows the borrower to transfer the balance of one or more high-interest credit card accounts to a new card with a lower interest rate.

What is an annual percentage rate (APR)?

The annual percentage rate (APR) is the annual rate of interest charged on a loan, expressed as a percentage of the loan amount.

What is a fixed interest rate loan?

A fixed interest rate loan is a loan in which the interest rate remains the same for the entire term of the loan.

What is a variable interest rate loan?

A variable interest rate loan is a loan in which the interest rate may fluctuate over the term of the loan, based on changes in market conditions.

What is a mortgage?

A mortgage is a loan used to purchase a property, with the property serving as collateral for the loan.

What is a home equity loan?

A home equity loan is a loan that is secured by the equity in a borrower's home, allowing the borrower to use the equity in their home as collateral for the loan.

What is a home equity line of credit (HELOC)?

A home equity line of credit (HELOC) is a loan in which the borrower can access funds up to a certain limit, using the equity in their home as collateral. The borrower can access the funds as needed, and only pays interest on the funds that are actually used.

What is an adjustable rate mortgage (ARM)?

An adjustable rate mortgage (ARM) is a type of mortgage in which the interest rate can fluctuate over the term of the loan, based on changes in market conditions.

What is a refinance?

Refinance is the process of paying off one loan with the proceeds from a new loan, typically with better terms or lower interest rate.

What is a car loan?

A car loan is a loan used to purchase a vehicle, with the vehicle serving as collateral for the loan.

What is a student loan?

A student loan is a loan used to pay for education-related expenses, such as tuition, books, and living expenses.

What is a 401(k) plan?

A 401(k) plan is a type of retirement savings plan offered by many employers, in which employees can save for retirement and often receive employer matching contributions.

What is an IRA (Individual Retirement Account)?

An IRA (Individual Retirement Account) is a type of personal savings plan used to save for retirement. There are several types of IRAs, including Traditional IRAs, Roth IRAs, and SEP IRAs.

What is a stock?

A stock is a type of security that represents ownership in a corporation. Stocks are often bought and sold on stock exchanges, and their value can fluctuate based on a variety of factors.

What is a bond?

A bond is a type of debt security in which an investor loans money to an organization, such as a corporation or government, in exchange for periodic interest payments and the return of the principal at the end of the bond's term.

What is a mutual fund?

A mutual fund is a type of investment vehicle in which a group of investors pool their money to purchase a diversified portfolio of stocks, bonds, or other securities.

What is an exchange-traded fund (ETF)?

An exchange-traded fund (ETF) is a type of investment fund that is traded on stock exchanges, similar to individual stocks. ETFs often track a specific market index, such as the S&P 500, and provide investors with a low-cost and diversified investment option.

What is a robo-advisor?

A robo-advisor is a type of digital investment service that uses algorithms and computer programs to provide investment advice and manage investment portfolios for clients.

What is a dividend?

A dividend is a payment made by a corporation to its shareholders, typically in the form of a cash distribution, based on the profits of the corporation.

What is a stock split?

A stock split is a corporate action in which a company increases the number of outstanding shares of its stock, while proportionally reducing the price per share.

What is a capital gain?

A capital gain is the profit realized from the sale of an investment, such as a stock or a real estate property, and is the difference between the purchase price and the sale price.

What is an interest rate swap?

An interest rate swap is a financial derivative in which two parties agree to exchange periodic interest payments on a specified loan or debt obligation. The interest rate swap is used to manage risk and hedge against changes in interest rates.

What is a foreign exchange rate?

A foreign exchange rate is the price at which one currency can be exchanged for another currency. Foreign exchange rates fluctuate based on a variety of economic and political factors, and are used to determine the value of one currency relative to another.

What is a money market fund?

A money market fund is a type of mutual fund that invests in short-term debt securities, such as Treasury bills and commercial paper, with the goal of providing a low-risk and stable investment option.

What is a credit rating?

A credit rating is an assessment of the creditworthiness of an individual or entity, based on their ability to repay debt. Credit ratings are often used by lenders and investors to determine the risk of lending money or investing in a particular borrower.

What is a credit score?

A credit score is a numerical representation of an individual's creditworthiness, based on their credit history and other financial factors. Credit scores are used by lenders to determine an individual's likelihood of repaying a loan and can impact the interest rates and loan terms they are offered.

What is a debit card?

A debit card is a type of payment card that is linked to an individual's checking account and can be used to make purchases or withdraw cash from an ATM. When a debit card is used, funds are automatically deducted from the linked checking account.

What is a credit card?

A credit card is a type of payment card that allows an individual to borrow money from a lender to make purchases or withdraw cash from an ATM. The individual must repay the borrowed funds, along with any associated interest and fees, to the lender.

What is a charge card?

A charge card is a type of credit card that requires the full balance to be paid at the end of each billing cycle, rather than allowing the borrower to carry a balance from month to month.

What is a prepaid card?

A prepaid card is a type of payment card that is loaded with a specific amount of funds, and can be used to make purchases or withdraw cash from an ATM until the funds are depleted.

What is a mobile banking app?

A mobile banking app is a digital application provided by a bank or financial institution that allows individuals to manage their financial accounts, including checking accounts, savings accounts, and credit cards, from their mobile devices.

What is electronic fund transfer (EFT)?

Electronic fund transfer (EFT) is a type of financial transaction that allows for the transfer of funds from one bank account to another through electronic means, without the use of physical checks or cash.

What is online banking?

Online banking is a type of banking service that allows individuals to manage their financial accounts, including checking accounts, savings accounts, and credit cards, through the internet using a computer or mobile device.

What is mobile banking?

Mobile banking is a type of banking service that allows individuals to manage their financial accounts, including checking accounts, savings accounts, and credit cards, through their mobile devices.

What is a wire transfer?

A wire transfer is a type of electronic fund transfer that allows for the transfer of funds from one bank account to another, often in real-time or within a few hours.

What is automatic bill payment?

Automatic bill payment is a type of banking service that allows individuals to set up recurring payments for bills, such as utility bills or credit card bills, to be automatically deducted from their bank account.

What is a direct deposit?

A direct deposit is a type of electronic fund transfer in which an employer or government agency deposits funds directly into an individual's bank account, without the need for physical checks or cash.

What is a standing order?

A standing order is a type of automatic payment that is set up between a bank and a customer, allowing for a fixed amount of money to be transferred from the customer's account to another account on a regular basis.

What is overdraft protection?

Overdraft protection is a type of banking service that allows individuals to overdraw their checking account up to a specified limit, without incurring overdraft fees or having transactions declined.

What is a certificate of deposit (CD)?

A certificate of deposit (CD) is a type of savings account in which an individual deposits a fixed amount of money for a set period of time, and earns a fixed rate of interest on the deposit.

What is a savings account?

A savings account is a type of bank account in which an individual deposits money for safekeeping and earns interest on the deposit. Savings accounts are typically used as a low-risk investment option for individuals looking to grow their savings over time.

What is a checking account?

A checking account is a type of bank account that allows individuals to deposit and withdraw funds, write checks, and make electronic transactions. Checking accounts are typically used for daily financial transactions and are linked to a debit card for easy access to funds.

What is a money market account?

A money market account is a type of savings account that typically pays higher interest rates than traditional savings accounts, but also requires a higher minimum balance. Money market accounts are designed for individuals looking for a low-risk investment option with higher returns.

What is a credit union?

A credit union is a type of financial institution that is owned and controlled by its members, and operates as a non-profit organization to provide financial services to its members. Credit unions typically offer a range of services, including savings accounts, checking accounts, loans, and credit cards.

What is a loan?

A loan is a type of financial product that allows an individual to borrow money from a lender, with the promise to repay the loan plus interest over a set period of time. Loans can be secured, such as with a mortgage, or unsecured, such as with a personal loan.

What is an interest rate?

An interest rate is the cost of borrowing money, expressed as a percentage of the amount borrowed. Interest rates can be fixed or variable, and determine the amount of money an individual will pay in interest over the life of the loan.

What is a fixed interest rate?

A fixed interest rate is an interest rate that remains constant for the life of the loan, regardless of changes in the market interest rates.

What is a variable interest rate?

A variable interest rate is an interest rate that can change over time, based on changes in the market interest rates.

What is an APR (Annual Percentage Rate)?

The APR (Annual Percentage Rate) is the total cost of borrowing money, expressed as a yearly interest rate. The APR includes not only the interest rate, but also any additional fees or charges associated with the loan.

What is a principal?

The principal is the amount of money borrowed, excluding any interest or fees.

What is amortization?

Amortization is the process of paying off a loan over time, through regular payments that include both principal and interest.

What is a collateral?

Collateral is a type of property or asset that is pledged as security for a loan, and can be seized by the lender if the borrower defaults on the loan.

What is a mortgage?

A mortgage is a type of loan used to finance the purchase of a property, such as a home. The property serves as collateral for the loan, and the borrower repays the loan plus interest over a set period of time.

What is a home equity loan?

A home equity loan is a type of loan that allows an individual to borrow against the equity in their home. The loan is secured by the home, and the amount of the loan is based on the value of the home minus any outstanding mortgage balances.

What is a credit score?

A credit score is a numerical representation of an individual's creditworthiness, based on their credit history and financial behavior. Credit scores are used by lenders to determine the risk of lending money to an individual, and can affect the interest rates and terms offered on loans and credit products.

What is a credit report?

A credit report is a detailed record of an individual's credit history, including information on credit accounts, payment history, and outstanding debts. Credit reports are used by lenders to determine an individual's creditworthiness and to make lending decisions.

What is a debit card?

A debit card is a type of payment card that allows individuals to make purchases or withdraw cash from their bank account. Debit cards are linked directly to an individual's checking account and transactions are deducted from the account balance in real-time.

What is a credit card?

A credit card is a type of payment card that allows individuals to make purchases or withdraw cash, up to a specified limit, without the need for immediate payment. Credit card transactions are paid for by the individual at a later date, typically with interest and fees added.

What is a balance transfer?

A balance transfer is a type of transaction in which an individual transfers the balance of one credit card to another credit card, typically to take advantage of lower interest rates or other promotional offers.

What is a cash advance?

A cash advance is a type of transaction in which an individual uses their credit card to withdraw cash from an ATM or other financial institution, typically incurring high fees and interest charges.

What is a revolving credit line?

A revolving credit line is a type of credit product that allows individuals to borrow and repay funds, up to a specified limit, on an ongoing basis. The borrowed amount and available credit line can fluctuate based on the individual's repayment history and borrowing behavior.

What is a money market account?

A money market account is a type of deposit account offered by financial institutions, offering higher interest rates than savings accounts and limited check-writing privileges. Money market accounts are meant for short-term savings and are typically FDIC-insured.

What is a mutual fund?

A mutual fund is a type of investment vehicle that pools money from multiple investors to purchase a diversified portfolio of securities, such as stocks, bonds, or real estate. Mutual funds are managed by professional fund managers, and offer a convenient way for individuals to invest in a diversified portfolio without having to purchase individual securities.

What is a real estate investment trust (REIT)?

A real estate investment trust (REIT) is a type of investment vehicle that invests in income-generating real estate properties, such as office buildings, apartments, or shopping centers. REITs offer individuals a way to invest in real estate without having to purchase and manage physical properties themselves.

What is a derivative?

A derivative is a financial instrument whose value is based on, or "derived" from, an underlying asset, such as a stock, bond, commodity, or currency. Derivatives are used for a variety of purposes, including hedging risk and speculating on market movements, and can take the form of options, futures, or swaps.

What is an annuity?

An annuity is a financial product that provides a stream of payments to an individual, typically in exchange for a lump sum payment or a series of payments. Annuities are used as a retirement income stream, and can be structured to provide a fixed or variable rate of return.

What is a swap?

A swap is a type of derivative in which two parties agree to exchange one stream of cash flows for another, based on an underlying asset such as a stock, bond, commodity, or currency. Swaps are used to manage risk or to speculate on market movements.

What is an option?

An option is a type of derivative that gives the holder the right, but not the obligation, to buy or sell an underlying asset at a specified price on or before a specified date. Options are used to hedge against price fluctuations or to speculate on future market movements.

What is a future contract?

A futures contract is a type of derivative in which two parties agree to buy or sell an underlying asset at a specified price on a specified date in the future. Futures contracts are used to hedge against price fluctuations or to speculate on future market movements.

What is a forward contract?

A forward contract is a type of derivative in which two parties agree to buy or sell an underlying asset at a specified price on a specified date in the future. Forward contracts are used to hedge against price fluctuations or to speculate on future market movements.

What is a pension plan?

A pension plan is a retirement savings plan offered by an employer, providing a guaranteed income stream to employees after they retire. Pension plans may be defined benefit plans, in which the employer guarantees a set benefit amount, or defined contribution plans, in which the employee's benefit is based on their contributions and investment performance.

What is a 401(k) plan?

A 401(k) plan is a type of defined contribution retirement savings plan offered by many employers, allowing employees to save and invest pre-tax dollars for their retirement. Employers may also offer matching contributions, boosting the employee's savings.

What is a Roth IRA?

A Roth IRA is a type of individual retirement account (IRA) that allows individuals to save and invest after-tax dollars for their retirement. Unlike traditional IRAs, Roth IRAs offer tax-free withdrawals in retirement, and there are no mandatory distribution age requirements.

What is a life insurance policy?

A life insurance policy is a contract between an individual and a life insurance company, in which the individual pays premiums in exchange for a death benefit. The death benefit is paid to the policy's beneficiaries upon the individual's death, and can be used to cover funeral expenses, outstanding debts, or to provide financial security for loved ones.

What is a health insurance policy?

A health insurance policy is a contract between an individual and a health insurance company, in which the individual pays premiums in exchange for coverage of certain medical expenses. Health insurance policies may cover a range of services, including doctor visits, hospital stays, and prescription drugs, and may be offered by employers or purchased individually.

What is an investment bank?

An investment bank is a financial institution that specializes in providing underwriting, advisory, and other financial services to large corporations and government entities. Investment banks help companies raise capital through the issuance of securities and also provide a range of services related to mergers and acquisitions, initial public offerings (IPOs), and other complex financial transactions.

What is a commercial bank?

A commercial bank is a type of financial institution that provides a range of banking services to individuals and businesses, including checking and savings accounts, loans, and other financial products. Commercial banks generate revenue by accepting deposits and making loans and investments, and by charging fees for services such as wire transfers and overdraft protection.

What is a savings and loan association?

A savings and loan association, also known as a savings and loan (S&L) or thrift, is a type of financial institution that specializes in accepting savings deposits and making mortgage loans. Savings and loan associations are typically structured as mutual organizations, owned by their depositors, and may offer higher interest rates on savings accounts than commercial banks.

What is a credit union?

A credit union is a type of financial cooperative owned and controlled by its members, typically offering a range of financial services including checking and savings accounts, loans, and other financial products. Credit unions are typically formed around a common bond, such as a shared workplace, community, or membership in a professional organization.

What is a money market fund?

A money market fund is a type of mutual fund that invests in short-term, low-risk debt instruments, such as government bonds, certificates of deposit (CDs), and commercial paper. Money market funds are typically considered to be a low-risk investment option, offering a higher rate of return than traditional savings accounts but with lower volatility than other types of investments.

What is a fixed deposit (FD)?

A fixed deposit (FD) is a type of savings account that allows individuals to deposit a fixed amount of money for a specified period of time, typically ranging from several months to several years. Fixed deposits typically offer a higher rate of return than traditional savings accounts, but the deposit is locked in for the term of the deposit and cannot be withdrawn without incurring a penalty.

What is a recurring deposit (RD)?

A recurring deposit (RD) is a type of savings account that allows individuals to make regular, fixed deposits into their account, typically on a monthly basis. Recurring deposits typically offer a higher rate of return than traditional savings accounts, and the deposit can be held for a specified term, such as 6 months, 1 year, or 2 years.

What is a bank rate?

A bank rate, also known as the discount rate, is the interest rate at which a central bank lends funds to commercial banks. The bank rate is a key tool used by central banks to influence the supply of money in the economy and to control inflation.

What is a repo rate?

A repo rate, also known as a repurchase agreement rate, is the interest rate at which a central bank lends funds to commercial banks by purchasing securities from them, with the agreement to sell the securities back at a later date. The repo rate is a key tool used by central banks to influence the supply of money in the economy and to control inflation.

What is an open market operation (OMO)?

An open market operation (OMO) is a type of monetary policy action taken by central banks to influence the supply of money in the economy. OMOs involve the purchase or sale of government securities in the open market, with the aim of increasing or decreasing the supply of money available for lending by commercial banks.

What is a base rate?

A base rate, also known as a benchmark rate, is a minimum interest rate set by a central bank for lending purposes, below which banks are not permitted to lend. The base rate serves as a benchmark for other interest rates in the economy and is used to help control inflation and maintain stability in the financial system. The base rate is typically reviewed and adjusted by central banks on a regular basis in response to changes in economic conditions.

What is a marginal cost of funds based lending rate (MCLR)?

A marginal cost of funds based lending rate (MCLR) is a system of determining the interest rate that commercial banks charge on their loans. MCLR is based on the marginal cost of funds, which takes into account the cost of borrowing funds and the cost of maintaining cash reserves. The MCLR system was introduced in India in 2016 to make the determination of interest rates more transparent and to ensure that changes in the cost of borrowing funds are reflected promptly in the interest rates charged by banks.

What is a prime lending rate?

A prime lending rate is the interest rate charged by banks on loans to their most creditworthy customers. The prime lending rate serves as a benchmark for other lending rates in the economy and is used as a reference point for determining the interest rate charged on loans to other customers. The prime lending rate is typically reviewed and adjusted by central banks on a regular basis in response to changes in economic conditions.

What is a floating rate loan?

A floating rate loan is a type of loan in which the interest rate charged on the loan varies in response to changes in a benchmark interest rate, such as the prime lending rate or the repo rate.

Floating rate loans offer borrowers the benefit of lower interest rates when benchmark rates fall, but also expose them to the risk of higher interest rates when benchmark rates rise.

What is a fixed rate loan?

A fixed rate loan is a type of loan in which the interest rate charged on the loan is fixed for the duration of the loan, regardless of changes in benchmark interest rates. Fixed rate loans offer borrowers the stability of a constant interest rate, but also limit their ability to take advantage of lower interest rates if benchmark rates fall.

What is an adjustable rate mortgage (ARM)?

An adjustable rate mortgage (ARM) is a type of mortgage in which the interest rate charged on the loan varies over time, in response to changes in a benchmark interest rate. ARMs offer borrowers the benefit of lower initial interest rates, but also expose them to the risk of higher interest rates in the future if benchmark rates rise.

What is a mortgage loan?

A mortgage loan is a type of loan used to purchase real estate, such as a house or a piece of land. Mortgage loans are typically secured by the property being purchased, and the loan amount is typically paid back over a period of several years, with the borrower making regular payments of principal and interest to the lender.

What is a collateral loan?

A collateral loan is a type of loan in which the borrower provides an asset, such as a car, jewelry, or real estate, as collateral for the loan. In the event of default, the lender may seize the collateral to recover the loan amount. Collateral loans typically offer higher loan amounts and more favorable terms than unsecured loans, but also carry the risk of losing the collateral in the event of default.

What is a secured loan?

A secured loan is a type of loan in which the borrower provides some type of collateral, such as a car or real estate, as security for the loan. In the event of default, the lender may seize the collateral to recover the loan amount. Secured loans typically offer higher loan amounts and more favorable terms than unsecured loans, but also carry the risk of losing the collateral in the event of default.

What is an unsecured loan?

An unsecured loan is a type of loan in which the borrower does not provide any collateral as security for the loan. Unsecured loans typically offer smaller loan amounts and less favorable terms than secured loans, but do not carry the risk of losing collateral in the event of default.

What is a consumer loan?

A consumer loan is a type of loan used to finance personal expenses, such as the purchase of a car, a home appliance, or a vacation. Consumer loans may be secured or unsecured, and may be offered by banks, credit unions, or other financial institutions.

What is a revolving credit facility?

A revolving credit facility is a type of loan in which the borrower has the ability to borrow and repay funds repeatedly, up to a certain maximum amount, without having to reapply for the loan each time. A revolving credit facility may be secured or unsecured, and may be offered by banks, credit unions, or other financial institutions.

What is a term loan?

A term loan is a type of loan in which the borrower receives a lump sum of money, and agrees to repay the loan over a set period of time, with regular payments of principal and interest. Term loans may be secured or unsecured, and may be offered by banks, credit unions, or other financial institutions.

What is a letter of credit?

A letter of credit is a document issued by a bank or other financial institution, guaranteeing payment to a seller in the event that the buyer is unable to fulfill its obligations under a contract. Letters of credit are often used in international trade transactions to provide a measure of protection for both the buyer and the seller.

What is a demand loan?

A demand loan is a type of loan in which the lender has the right to demand repayment of the loan at any time, without giving the borrower prior notice. Demand loans are often used for short-term financing needs and may be offered by banks, credit unions, or other financial institutions.

What is a structured finance transaction?

A structured finance transaction is a type of financing in which the risk of a loan or a portfolio of loans is divided into separate tranches, with each tranche having its own level of risk and return. Structured finance transactions are often used to raise capital for large and complex financing needs, such as infrastructure projects or real estate developments.

What is a collateralized debt obligation (CDO)?

A collateralized debt obligation (CDO) is a type of structured finance transaction in which a pool of debt securities, such as mortgages or corporate bonds, is combined and repackaged into new securities. The new securities are then sold to investors, with each tranche having a different level of risk and return based on the underlying debt securities.

What is a mortgage-backed security (MBS)?

A mortgage-backed security (MBS) is a type of security in which a pool of mortgages is combined and repackaged into new securities that are sold to investors. The cash flows from the underlying mortgages are used to make periodic payments to MBS investors. MBS are commonly used to raise capital for residential and commercial real estate lending.

What is an asset-backed security (ABS)?

An asset-backed security (ABS) is a type of security in which a pool of assets, such as auto loans or credit card receivables, is combined and repackaged into new securities that are sold to investors. The cash flows from the underlying assets are used to make periodic payments to ABS investors. ABS are commonly used to raise capital for consumer and small business lending.

What is a commercial paper?

Commercial paper is a type of short-term debt security issued by corporations and financial institutions. Commercial paper typically has maturities of less than 270 days and is used to finance short-term borrowing needs, such as working capital requirements or inventory financing.

What is a municipal bond?

A municipal bond is a type of bond issued by state and local governments to finance public projects, such as schools, roads, and bridges. Municipal bonds are generally considered to be safe investments, as they are backed by the creditworthiness of the issuing government.

What is a Treasury bond?

A Treasury bond is a type of bond issued by the federal government to finance its spending needs. Treasury bonds are considered to be among the safest investments, as they are backed by the full faith and credit of the US government.

What is a corporate bond?

A corporate bond is a type of bond issued by a corporation to finance its business operations. Corporate bonds are considered to be riskier investments than Treasury bonds, as they are dependent on the financial performance and creditworthiness of the issuing corporation.

What is a junk bond?

A junk bond, also known as a high-yield bond, is a type of bond issued by companies with low credit ratings, or by companies in industries with high default risk, such as energy or mining. Junk bonds offer higher yields than investment-grade bonds, but also carry higher default risk.

What is a credit rating?

A credit rating is a measure of the creditworthiness of an issuer, such as a corporation or government, based on its ability to repay its debts. Credit ratings are assigned by credit rating agencies, such as Moody's or Standard & Poor's, and range from AAA (highest) to D (default).

What is a credit spread?

A credit spread is the difference in yield between a benchmark security, such as a Treasury bond, and a similarly-matured security with a lower credit rating. Credit spreads are used to measure the risk premium associated with lending to a less creditworthy issuer.

What is a yield curve?

A yield curve is a graph that plots the yields of similar securities with different maturities. Yield curves are used to compare the yields of securities with different maturities, and to track changes in interest rate expectations over time.

What is a bull market?

A bull market is a market characterized by a prolonged period of rising prices. In a bull market, investors are optimistic about the future and are willing to pay higher prices for securities, leading to overall market gains.

What is a bear market?

A bear market is a market characterized by a prolonged period of declining prices. In a bear market, investors are pessimistic about the future and are selling off securities, leading to overall market losses.

What is a market correction?

A market correction is a short-term decline in the price of securities, typically defined as a drop of at least 10% from recent highs. Market corrections are a normal part of market cycles and are typically seen as a healthy development, as they can help to alleviate market bubbles and reset valuations to more reasonable levels.

What is a recession?

A recession is a period of economic contraction, characterized by declining output, employment, and trade. Recessions are typically identified by two consecutive quarters of negative gross domestic product (GDP) growth.

What is inflation?

Inflation is a measure of the rate at which the general level of prices for goods and services is rising, and thus, purchasing power is falling. Inflation is typically measured by the Consumer Price Index (CPI) or the Producer Price Index (PPI).

What is a deflation?

Deflation is a measure of the rate at which the general level of prices for goods and services is falling, and thus, purchasing power is increasing. Deflation can be harmful to an economy, as it can lead to lower consumer spending and investment, and can make debt more difficult to repay.

What is monetary policy?

Monetary policy is the process by which a central bank, such as the Federal Reserve, manages the supply of money in an economy in order to achieve its macroeconomic goals, such as low inflation and high employment. Monetary policy is typically conducted through the use of tools such as interest rates, reserve requirements, and open market operations.

What is fiscal policy?

Fiscal policy is the process by which a government manages its spending and revenue in order to achieve its macroeconomic goals, such as low inflation and high employment. Fiscal policy can be expansionary, meaning that the government increases spending or lowers taxes in order to stimulate the economy, or it can be contractionary, meaning that the government reduces spending or raises taxes in order to slow down the economy.

What is Gross Domestic Product (GDP)?

Gross Domestic Product (GDP) is the total value of goods and services produced within a country's borders in a given period of time, usually one year. GDP is used as a measure of a country's overall economic output and is considered a key indicator of the health of an economy.

What is Gross National Product (GNP)?

Gross National Product (GNP) is the total value of goods and services produced by a country's residents, regardless of where they are located, in a given period of time, usually one year. GNP is used as a measure of a country's overall economic output, including both domestic production and foreign production by its residents.

What is the Consumer Price Index (CPI)?

The Consumer Price Index (CPI) is a measure of the average change in prices over time for a basket of goods and services purchased by consumers. The CPI is used as a measure of inflation and is used by the Federal Reserve to help determine monetary policy.

What is the Producer Price Index (PPI)?

The Producer Price Index (PPI) is a measure of the average change in prices received by domestic producers for their output. The PPI is used as a measure of inflation at the wholesale level and is a leading indicator of consumer inflation.

What is the current account balance?

The current account balance is a measure of a country's net trade in goods and services, as well as transfers such as remittances and foreign aid. A positive current account balance means that a country is exporting more goods and services than it is importing, while a negative current account balance means that a country is importing more goods and services than it is exporting.

What is the capital account balance?

The capital account balance is a measure of a country's net transactions in financial assets, such as stocks, bonds, and foreign direct investment. A positive capital account balance means that a country is attracting more foreign investment than it is losing, while a negative capital account balance means that a country is losing more foreign investment than it is attracting.

What is foreign direct investment (FDI)?

Foreign direct investment (FDI) is an investment made by a company or individual in one country into a company or entity based in another country. FDI can take the form of building new facilities, acquiring existing businesses, or investing in long-term assets.

What is a trade surplus?

A trade surplus is a situation in which a country exports more goods and services than it imports, resulting in a positive balance of trade.

What is a trade deficit?

A trade deficit is a situation in which a country imports more goods and services than it exports, resulting in a negative balance of trade.

What is the foreign exchange market?

The foreign exchange market, also known as the forex market, is a decentralized market where currencies are traded. The foreign exchange market is the largest financial market in the world, with an average daily trading volume of over $5 trillion.

What is an exchange rate?

An exchange rate is the value of one currency in terms of another currency. Exchange rates can be quoted as the value of one currency per unit of another currency, or as the value of one currency in terms of a basket of other currencies.

What is the role of the central bank in the foreign exchange market?

The central bank plays a significant role in the foreign exchange market by setting and implementing monetary policy, which can affect the demand for a country's currency and therefore its exchange rate. The central bank can also intervene in the foreign exchange market to buy or sell its currency in order to influence the exchange rate.

What is currency appreciation?

Currency appreciation is a situation in which the value of a currency increases relative to another currency or basket of currencies. This can occur due to a variety of factors, including an increase in demand for the currency, a decrease in supply of the currency, or a positive change in the economic conditions of the country issuing the currency.

What is currency depreciation?

Currency depreciation is a situation in which the value of a currency decreases relative to another currency or basket of currencies. This can occur due to a variety of factors, including a decrease in demand for the currency, an increase in supply of the currency, or a negative change in the economic conditions of the country issuing the currency.

What is a currency peg?

A currency peg is a situation in which a country's central bank sets a fixed exchange rate between its currency and another currency or basket of currencies. The central bank may then intervene in the foreign exchange market to buy or sell its currency in order to maintain the pegged exchange rate.

What is a floating exchange rate?

A floating exchange rate is a situation in which the value of a currency is determined by supply and demand in the foreign exchange market, without intervention from the central bank. The exchange rate can fluctuate in response to changes in economic conditions and market forces.

What is the purpose of a central bank?

The purpose of a central bank is to manage a country's monetary policy and provide financial services to the government. Central banks also play a role in maintaining the stability of the financial system, managing the supply of money in the economy, and serving as the lender of last resort in times of financial crisis.

What is monetary policy?

Monetary policy is the process by which a central bank manages the supply of money in the economy in order to achieve its macroeconomic objectives, such as low inflation, full employment, and stable economic growth. Monetary policy can be conducted through a variety of tools, including setting interest rates, adjusting reserve requirements, and engaging in open market operations.

What is the difference between nominal and real interest rates?

Nominal interest rates are expressed in current dollars, while real interest rates are adjusted for changes in the price level, expressed in constant dollars. Real interest rates reflect the true cost of borrowing, taking into account inflation.

CHAPTER SIX

Banking Terminology Glossary

ATM: Automated Teller Machine

ACH: Automated Clearing House

BSB: Bank-State-Branch Number

CD: Certificate of Deposit

Debit card: A card that deducts money directly from a consumer's checking account

Direct deposit: A payment method where funds are transferred electronically into an account

EFT: Electronic Fund Transfer

FDIC: Federal Deposit Insurance Corporation

FICO: Fair Isaac Corporation

IBAN: International Bank Account Number

KYC: Know Your Customer

Loan: An amount of money borrowed

Mortage: A loan used to buy real estate

NSF: Non-Sufficient Funds

PIN: Personal Identification Number

Savings account: A deposit account that pays interest on savings

SWIFT: Society for Worldwide Interbank Financial Telecommunication

Wire transfer: An electronic transfer of funds from one bank to another

YTD: Year-to-Date.

Interest rate: The cost of borrowing money, expressed as a percentage

Credit score: A numerical representation of an individual's creditworthiness

APR: Annual Percentage Rate

Collateral: Property or assets pledged as security for a loan

Principal: The original amount of a loan or deposit

Capital: Total assets minus liabilities

Reserve requirements: The amount of funds that a bank must hold in reserve

Balance: The difference between a person's assets and liabilities

Overdraft: A situation where an account holder spends more money than they have in their account

Reconciliation: The process of comparing two sets of records to ensure accuracy

Endorsement: A signature on the back of a check that endorses its validity

Depository: A place where funds are deposited

Clearing house: An institution that facilitates the exchange of information between banks

Liquidity: The ability of an asset to be quickly converted into cash without significant loss of value.

Fractional reserve banking: A banking system in which banks hold only a fraction of their deposits in reserve, lending out the rest

Derivatives: Financial products whose value is based on an underlying asset

Hedge fund: An investment fund that uses various strategies to generate high returns

Leverage: The use of borrowed money to increase investment returns

Margin: The amount of money required to be deposited as collateral when trading securities on margin

Speculation: Investing in an asset with the expectation of making a profit based on price movements

Diversification: Spreading investments across different asset classes to reduce risk

Asset: Something valuable that an individual, corporation, or country owns

Liability: Something owed to another person or entity

Bond: A debt security in which the issuer owes the holder a debt and is obliged to pay interest

Stock: A type of security that signifies ownership in a corporation and represents a claim on part of the corporation's assets and earnings.

IPO: Initial Public Offering, the first time a company's stock becomes available for public trading

Mutual fund: An investment vehicle that pools money from many investors to purchase securities

Portfolio: A collection of investments held by an individual or institution

Index fund: A type of mutual fund that tracks a market index, such as the S&P 500

ETF: Exchange-Traded Fund, a type of investment fund that is traded on stock exchanges like individual stocks

ROI: Return on Investment, a measure of the profit earned on an investment relative to the investment's cost.

Capital gains: The profit made from the sale of a capital asset, such as stock or real estate

Capital loss: The loss incurred from the sale of a capital asset, such as stock or real estate

Market capitalization: The total value of a company's outstanding shares of stock

Dividend: A portion of a company's profits paid out to shareholders

Blue-chip stock: Stock of a well-established and financially sound company with a history of stability and steady growth

Growth stock: Stock of a company that is expected to grow at a faster rate than the overall market.

Value stock: Stock of a company that is considered undervalued in comparison to its earnings and growth potential

Risk tolerance: An individual's willingness to accept fluctuations in the value of their investments in pursuit of higher returns

Market risk: The risk that an investment's value will decline due to changes in the overall market

Credit risk: The risk that a borrower will default on a loan or debt obligation.

Inflation risk: The risk that the purchasing power of money will decline over time

Political risk: The risk that a government action or decision will have a negative impact on an investment

Currency risk: The risk that an investment's value will change due to fluctuations in exchange rates

Liquidity risk: The risk that an investor will be unable to convert an asset into cash quickly enough to avoid a loss

Systematic risk: The risk that affects an entire market, rather than a specific security or sector

Unsystematic risk: The risk that is specific to a particular security or sector and can be diversified away through proper portfolio management.

Alpha: A measure of an investment's performance relative to a benchmark index

Beta: A measure of an investment's volatility compared to the overall market

Correlation: A statistical measure of the relationship between two securities or sets of data

Standard deviation: A measure of the amount by which an investment's returns vary from its average return.

Yield: The income generated by an investment, expressed as a percentage of its cost

Coupon rate: The interest rate paid on a fixed-income security, such as a bond

Maturity: The date when a bond will be redeemed and the principal repaid to the investor

Call option: A financial contract that gives the holder the right, but not the obligation, to buy an underlying asset at a specified price

Put option: A financial contract that gives the holder the right, but not the obligation, to sell an underlying asset at a specified price.

Strike price: The specified price at which an option can be exercised

Expiration date: The date after which an option is no longer valid

Option premium: The price of an option, paid by the buyer to the seller

Hedging: An investment strategy used to reduce the risk of loss from market fluctuations

Financial advisor: A professional who provides advice and guidance on investments and financial planning.

Wealth management: A comprehensive approach to managing an individual's financial affairs, including investments, retirement planning, tax planning, and estate planning

Estate planning: The process of organizing and arranging one's assets and finances to be passed on to beneficiaries after death

Tax planning: The process of organizing and arranging one's finances in a way that minimizes tax liability

Retirement planning: The process of planning and saving for one's financial needs during retirement.

Endowment: A sum of money or property donated to an institution, such as a university, with the intention that the income generated by the endowment be used to support specific activities

Annuity: A financial product that provides a stream of income payments at regular intervals, typically in exchange for a lump sum payment

Pension: A retirement plan that provides a defined benefit to an employee upon retirement

Social Security: A government-sponsored program that provides retirement, disability, and survivors' benefits to eligible individuals

401(k): A type of employer-sponsored retirement savings plan.

IRA: Individual Retirement Account, a type of savings account designed specifically for retirement savings.

Roth IRA: A type of individual retirement account in which contributions are made on an after-tax basis, and qualified withdrawals are tax-free

529 plan: A tax-advantaged savings plan designed to encourage saving for future education expenses

Trust: A legal arrangement in which a trustee holds and manages property for the benefit of another person

Will: A legal document that outlines how an individual's assets will be distributed after death

Power of attorney: A legal document that gives another person the authority to act on one's behalf in financial or legal matters.

Guardianship: A legal relationship in which a guardian is appointed to make decisions and take care of a minor or a person who is unable to make decisions for themselves

Estate tax: A tax on the transfer of an individual's estate at death

Gift tax: A tax on the transfer of money or property to another person as a gift

Capital gains tax: A tax on the profit made from the sale of a capital asset

Income tax: A tax on an individual's or corporation's taxable income.

Deduction: An expense that can be subtracted from one's taxable income to reduce the amount of tax owed

Credit: A reduction in the amount of tax owed

Refinance: The process of obtaining a new loan to pay off an existing loan or other debt

Foreclosure: The legal process by which a lender takes possession of a property when the borrower is unable to repay a loan

Escrow: A process in which a neutral third party holds and manages funds or property on behalf of another party

Deed: A legal document that transfers ownership of real property from one person to another.

Closing costs: The expenses incurred in the process of buying or selling a property, including fees for title searches, legal services, and recording charges

Property tax: A tax on real property, such as a house or land

Homeowners insurance: An insurance policy that covers the structure of a home and its contents against damage or loss

Mortgage: A loan used to purchase a property, with the property serving as collateral for the loan.

Principal: The amount borrowed or the amount still owed on a loan

Interest: The fee charged by a lender for the use of money, typically expressed as a percentage of the loan amount

Loan-to-value ratio: A ratio that compares the amount of a loan to the value of the property being purchased

Amortization: The process of paying off a loan in regular payments over time

Fixed-rate mortgage: A mortgage with an interest rate that remains constant for the life of the loan

Adjustable-rate mortgage: A mortgage with an interest rate that can change over time, typically tied to an index

Balloon mortgage: A mortgage with a large payment due at the end of the loan term.

FHA loan: A loan insured by the Federal Housing Administration, designed to help low- and moderate-income individuals obtain financing for a home purchase

VA loan: A loan guaranteed by the Department of Veterans Affairs, designed to help eligible veterans obtain financing for a home purchase

Jumbo loan: A loan that exceeds the conforming loan limit set by government-sponsored entities such as Fannie Mae and Freddie Mac.

Zero-down mortgage: A mortgage program that allows borrowers to purchase a home with no down payment required

Cash-out refinance: A type of refinance transaction in which the borrower receives cash from the equity in their home

Home equity loan: A loan that allows a homeowner to borrow against the equity in their home

Home equity line of credit: A line of credit that allows a homeowner to borrow against the equity in their home

Reverse mortgage: A type of loan that allows a homeowner to access the equity in their home, with no required monthly payments.

Short sale: A sale of a property in which the proceeds from the sale are less than the amount owed on the mortgage

Foreclosure alternative: Programs or processes designed to help homeowners avoid foreclosure, such as loan modification, short sale, or deed in lieu of foreclosure

Credit score: A numerical representation of an individual's creditworthiness, based on their credit history and other factors

Credit report: A record of an individual's credit history, including information about their payment history, credit accounts, and other factors

Credit bureau: A company that collects and maintains credit information on individuals and provides it to lenders and other entities.

FICO score: A widely used credit score developed by the Fair Isaac Corporation

Debt-to-income ratio: A ratio that compares an individual's debt payments to their gross monthly income

Collateral: Property or assets pledged as security for a loan

Cosigner: A person who signs a loan agreement with the borrower and agrees to repay the loan if the borrower defaults

Repossess: To take back possession of property that was used as collateral for a loan

Default: Failure to repay a loan according to the terms agreed upon in the loan agreement

Secured loan: A loan that is secured by collateral.

Unsecured loan: A loan that is not secured by collateral

Personal loan: An unsecured loan for personal use, such as for debt consolidation or home improvements

Payday loan: A short-term, high-interest loan that is typically due on the borrower's next payday.

Line of credit: A pre-approved loan amount that a borrower can access as needed

Overdraft: A situation in which a bank allows a customer to withdraw more funds than are available in their account

Overdraft fee: A fee charged by a bank when a customer overdrafts their account

Bounce check: A check that is returned by a bank due to insufficient funds in the account

Direct deposit: A method of depositing funds directly into a bank account, without the need for a physical check

Electronic funds transfer (EFT): A transfer of funds from one bank account to another that is conducted electronically.

Automated Clearing House (ACH): An electronic network for processing transactions, including direct deposit and electronic bill payments

Wire transfer: An electronic transfer of funds from one bank to another

Debit card: A card that allows the holder to access funds in a checking account for purchases and cash withdrawals

Credit card: A card that allows the holder to borrow money from the issuer to make purchases, with the option to pay back the loan over time.

Balance transfer: A transaction that moves debt from one credit card to another

Annual percentage rate (APR): The annual interest rate charged on a loan, expressed as a percentage

Minimum payment: The minimum amount due on a credit card or loan each month

Late fee: A fee charged by a lender when a payment is received after the due date

Grace period: A period of time after the due date during which a payment can be made without incurring a late fee

Credit limit: The maximum amount that a borrower can spend on a credit card.

Rewards program: A program offered by credit card issuers that allows cardholders to earn rewards for using their card, such as cash back or points

Secured credit card: A credit card that requires a deposit to be made as collateral

Unsecured credit card: A credit card that does not require a deposit to be made as collateral

Charge off: A debt that is considered uncollectable by the lender and is written off as a loss on their books.

Debt management plan: A plan to repay debt through a structured repayment schedule

Debt consolidation loan: A loan that is used to pay off multiple debts, resulting in a single monthly payment

Debt settlement: A negotiation between a borrower and their creditors to repay a portion of the debt owed in exchange for a release of the remaining debt

Credit counseling: A service that provides education and support for individuals seeking to manage their debt

Bankruptcy: A legal process in which a person's debts are discharged or reorganized.

Chapter 7 bankruptcy: A type of bankruptcy in which the person's assets are sold to repay their creditors

Chapter 13 bankruptcy: A type of bankruptcy in which the person repays their debts over a period of three to five years

Liquidation: The process of selling assets in order to pay off debts

Garnishment: The legal process of deducting money from a person's wages to repay a debt

Foreclosure: The legal process in which a lender takes possession of a property because the borrower has defaulted on their mortgage.

Escrow: A neutral third-party that holds funds or property during a transaction, to be released when certain conditions are met

Title insurance: An insurance policy that protects the owner of a property from losses arising from disputes over ownership of the property

Closing costs: The costs associated with buying or selling a property, such as title search fees, appraisal fees, and loan origination fees

Home equity loan: A loan that is secured by the equity in a borrower's home

Refinance: The process of obtaining a new loan to pay off an existing loan

Fixed-rate mortgage: A mortgage with an interest rate that remains fixed over the life of the loan.

Adjustable-rate mortgage (ARM): A mortgage with an interest rate that can change over time, based on changes in a specified index

Interest-only loan: A loan in which the borrower pays only the interest on the loan for a specified period of time, before beginning to repay the principal

Balloon loan: A loan in which a large payment is due at the end of the loan term, in addition to the regular monthly payments

Reverse mortgage: A loan that allows a homeowner to borrow against the equity in their home, typically used as a source of retirement income.

Investment portfolio: A collection of investments, such as stocks, bonds, and real estate, that are held by an individual or institution

Asset allocation: The process of dividing an investment portfolio among different asset classes, such as stocks, bonds, and cash, in order to diversify risk

Diversification: The strategy of spreading investments among multiple assets to reduce the overall risk of the portfolio

Risk tolerance: An individual's willingness to accept potential losses in their investment portfolio in pursuit of higher returns.

Mutual fund: A type of investment vehicle that pools money from multiple investors to purchase a diversified portfolio of stocks, bonds, or other securities

Exchange-traded fund (ETF): A type of investment fund that tracks an index, such as the S&P 500, and is traded on an exchange like a stock

Stock: A type of security that represents ownership in a corporation

Bond: A type of security that represents a loan made by an investor to a borrower, such as a corporation or government

Real estate investment trust (REIT): A type of investment vehicle that invests in income-producing real estate properties.

Capital gains: The profit realized from the sale of an investment, such as a stock or real estate property.

Capital loss: The loss realized from the sale of an investment, such as a stock or real estate property.

Dividends: Payments made to shareholders of a corporation, typically from the company's profits

Yield: The return on an investment, expressed as a percentage of the investment's cost

Compound interest: Interest that is calculated not only on the original amount invested, but also on the accumulated interest over time

Annuity: A type of investment that provides regular payments, typically for a specified period of time

401(k): A type of employer-sponsored retirement savings plan in the United States.

IRA: An individual retirement account that allows individuals to save for retirement on a tax-advantaged basis

Roth IRA: A type of individual retirement account that is funded with after-tax dollars and allows for tax-free withdrawals in retirement

Social Security: A federal insurance program in the United States that provides retirement, disability, and survivor benefits to eligible individuals

Pension plan: A type of retirement plan in which an employer makes contributions to a pool of funds set aside for the benefit of employees.

Capital market: A market for trading long-term debt or equity-backed securities

Primary market: The market where new securities are issued and sold to investors for the first time

Secondary market: The market where securities that have been previously issued are bought and sold

Underwriting: The process of evaluating the creditworthiness of a borrower and assuming the risk of issuing a loan or security

Initial public offering (IPO): The process by which a company first becomes publicly traded by issuing new shares of stock to the public.

Stock exchange: A marketplace where stocks and other securities are traded

Market capitalization: The total value of a company's outstanding shares of stock

Blue-chip stocks: Stocks of well-established, financially stable companies with a history of strong performance

Growth stock: Stock of a company that is expected to grow at a faster rate than the overall market

Value stock: Stock of a company that is considered undervalued based on its earnings, assets, or future growth prospects.

Bear market: A market condition characterized by declining security prices

Bull market: A market condition characterized by rising security prices

Correction: A temporary reversal in the price trend of a security or the overall market

Dividend yield: The annual dividend payment of a stock, expressed as a percentage of the stock's price

Earnings per share (EPS): The portion of a company's profit allocated to each outstanding share of common stock

Price to earnings ratio (P/E ratio): The ratio of a company's stock price to its earnings per share, used to evaluate the company's current stock price relative to its earnings.

Gross domestic product (GDP): The total value of goods and services produced within a country's borders in a given time period

Inflation: An increase in the general level of prices of goods and services in an economy over a period of time

Monetary policy: The actions taken by a central bank to control the supply of money in an economy and achieve macroeconomic goals such as inflation control and full employment

Fiscal policy: The actions taken by a government to influence the level of economic activity and manage the economy, such as taxes, spending, and regulation.

Balance of payments: A record of all transactions between a country and the rest of the world over a certain period of time

Current account: A component of the balance of payments that includes all trade in goods and services and transfer payments

Capital account: A component of the balance of payments that includes all investments and capital transfers

Foreign direct investment (FDI): An investment made by a company or individual in a foreign country, such as the purchase of a foreign company or the establishment of a new business

Exchange rate: The value of one currency in terms of another currency.

Floating exchange rate: An exchange rate system in which the value of a currency is determined by market forces and can fluctuate freely

Fixed exchange rate: An exchange rate system in which the value of a currency is fixed relative to another currency or basket of currencies

Currency appreciation: An increase in the value of a currency in terms of another currency.

Currency depreciation: A decrease in the value of a currency in terms of another currency.

CHAPTER SEVEN

Conclusion:

In conclusion, this book has provided a comprehensive guide to the most frequently asked questions in banking interviews. From general questions about the banking industry and your experiences, to technical questions about finance, accounting, and economics, the book has covered a wide range of topics to help you prepare for your interview.

By familiarizing yourself with the common questions and considering the suggested answers, you will be able to demonstrate your knowledge, skills, and confidence during your interview. Remember to also tailor your responses to fit the specific bank and position you are applying for, and to highlight your unique strengths and qualifications.

Best of luck with your interview, and we hope this book has been a valuable resource in your journey to securing a job in the banking industry.

CHAPTER EIGHT

Final Thoughts

In the final thoughts of this book on banking interview questions and answers, it is important to emphasize the value of preparation and practice. While this book provides a comprehensive guide to the most common questions, it is just one part of your preparation process.

It is essential to also research the specific bank you are interviewing with and the position you are applying for, and to familiarize yourself with the company culture, values, and goals. You may also consider mock interviews with friends, family, or a career coach to get a feel for the interview process and receive constructive feedback on your responses.

Remember to always be yourself during the interview and to showcase your passion for the banking industry and your eagerness to contribute to the success of the bank. With proper preparation, a confident attitude, and a solid understanding of the industry and the role you are applying for, you will be well on your way to securing a job in the competitive world of banking.

CHAPTER NINE

Next Steps for Your Career in Banking

The next steps will depend on your current situation and career goals, but here are a few suggestions to help you move forward:

Network and Build Relationships: Networking can play a crucial role in advancing your career in banking. Attend industry events, join professional organizations, and connect with colleagues, alumni, and mentors to build relationships and learn about new opportunities.

Continue Your Education: Banking is a constantly evolving industry, and it is essential to stay up to date with the latest developments and best practices. Consider taking courses, attending workshops, or obtaining certifications to enhance your skills and knowledge.

Seek Out Opportunities for Growth: Whether it is through job rotations, cross-functional projects, or leadership programs, look for opportunities within your current organization or outside of it to develop new skills, gain experience, and take on new challenges.

Set Career Goals: Identify your career goals and create a plan to achieve them. Consider what skills and experience you need to acquire, what kind of job you want to have, and what kind of impact you want to make in the industry.

Be Open to Change: The banking industry is constantly evolving, and it is essential to be open to change and adapt to new developments. Be willing to embrace new technologies, business models, and processes to stay ahead of the curve.

By following these steps, you will be well on your way to a successful and fulfilling career in banking. Remember to always be proactive, stay focused on your goals, and never stop learning and growing. Good luck!

Thank You

Printed by Libri Plureos GmbH in Hamburg,
Germany